Objective Testing

Objective Testing

H. G. Macintosh, M.A.
Associated Examining Board

R. B. Morrison, B.Sc., Ph.D., A.K.C.
School of Education, University of Reading

University of London Press Ltd

SBN 340 09580 6 Boards
SBN 340 09643 8 Unibook

University of London Press Ltd
St Paul's House, Warwick Lane, London EC4

Printed and bound in Great Britain by
Hazell Watson & Viney Ltd, Aylesbury, Bucks

Contents

Preface

Much of the material used in this survey of objective testing originated from papers prepared for committees concerned with new techniques of examining (HGM), and from courses in educational measurement for teachers and education students (RBM). The book thus reflects a concern for the development of objective tests within the framework of the existing examination structure, and an awareness of the current interest in new techniques of assessment in education.

It is important to make two general points about the book. First, it is designed primarily for the teacher, particularly the teacher in the secondary school, although it is hoped that the general reader will also find it of interest. We have aimed to provide, with a minimum of jargon and technical detail, information about a form of testing which pupils in the schools are likely to take increasingly in the future and which teachers might like to develop for classroom use. Secondly, the book has been written at a time when the use of objective tests in the United Kingdom is in its infancy and when expert knowledge is limited. It is, moreover, a time when the character of public examinations is rapidly changing and when many new techniques of assessment are being tried out. Objective testing is but one of these new techniques. The book is designed, therefore, as an introduction to the subject, and it is hoped that it might encourage the reader to find out about the subject in more detail. Some suggestions for further reading are provided at the end of the book.

The sample items used in this book have been taken in the main from the subject areas of history and physics, although the principles discussed apply to all subjects. In considering items, however, it is essential to stress the point which is the concern

7

of the concluding chapter, namely, that no consideration of test items or testing techniques can be divorced from the discussion of educational objectives. Such objectives need to be established and defined in relation to a particular test in a particular subject for a particular group of pupils. The examples used should therefore be regarded as illustrating item types, and not necessarily as being appropriate for use in any specific test.

It would be impossible to acknowledge all the help and advice which many people have given so generously. We should, however, particularly like to thank the following: the Associated Examining Board and its Secretary, B. C. Lucia; Educational Testing Service, Princeton, New Jersey; the Psychological Corporation, New York; University of London School Examinations Council; G. K. Bennett, R. L. Ebel, E. F. Lindquist, F. M. Ottobre, L. A. Smith and W. L. Wallace. Lastly, we should like to thank Miss B. Copping and Miss C. Rush for all their hard work in typing the manuscript.

H. G. Macintosh
R. B. Morrison
October 1968

CHAPTER I

The objective test

An objective test is one in which the questions, or 'items' as they are usually called, are asked in such a way that for each of them there is only one predetermined correct answer. It follows, therefore, that subjectivity in the marking or scoring of the test is eliminated and that it can be marked by an individual without any knowledge of the subject, or by a specially designed scoring machine. Nevertheless, even in an objective test there are degrees of objectivity; this is a point which will be illustrated in more detail later when varieties of item types are discussed. However, we can in general say that items which ask the candidate to select an answer from a given list are completely objective as far as scoring is concerned, while those which ask him to supply an answer are only partially objective. The reader will note the phrase 'objective as far as scoring is concerned'. It is not suggested for one moment that the subjective element has been eliminated altogether in an objective test. Subjective decisions have to be taken in the preparation of the specifications for any test—for example, in the content to be covered and in the abilities or skills to be tested. But, even here, the subjective element is less than it is in the majority of existing tests, particularly the widely used external essay test. As will be seen later, an objective test, if properly constructed, involves many more people than an essay test does. Moreover, the objective test contains many items and thus the content coverage is wider.

It will be noted that we have used the word 'test' and not 'examination' in the opening sentence. An artificial distinction has developed in the United Kingdom between the two words, which reflects a failure to consider testing as a unified whole. Instead, we try to break it down into categories which at times are regarded as watertight, as, for example, 'achievement examinations' and 'aptitude tests'. This distinction seems to be largely meaningless, and the use of the word 'test' would seem therefore to be more appropriate.

To many people it seems horrifying that a test paper which represents the end of a long programme of hard work should be marked by a machine or an unskilled clerk. The fact that this is a commonly held point of view reflects our greater familiarity with essay tests. With essay tests, although great care is taken in setting the questions, the major effort is expended upon their marking; and this is usually carried out by qualified and experienced teachers. With an objective test, on the other hand, the major effort is expended on the setting (which is all-important), and comparatively little effort is spent on the marking. Provided the items have been properly constructed and ambiguity has been avoided, the marker has only to be able to read the correct answers from a key and to add up the total score at the end. For this task an optical scanning machine is likely to be more accurate, since it does not suffer from fatigue when repeating routine procedures. The latest machines are provided with various checks—the procedure being given the general name of 'quality control'—which further ensures accuracy without any sacrifice of speed.

The marking or scoring of an objective test is made even easier by the normal practice of awarding one mark to each and every item, regardless of its difficulty. While this is valuable for speed and ease of marking, it may well cause concern. Why should the answer to an item testing a more difficult aspect of the subject, to which more thought has been given by the candidate, receive the same marks as a much easier item? Surely such a procedure can only penalise the better candidate! To this very reasonable concern there are two answers: first, an objective test consists not of a few items but of a substantial number, all of which should be attempted; secondly, in an objective test it is possible to work out the degree of difficulty of any item in advance by trying it out upon a group similar in age, type of school and educational background to those who will be taking the test proper. In this way a test can be constructed which is pitched at a level of difficulty that will enable the better candidate to show his ability by achieving a higher score on the test as a whole, and, at the same time, give the average candidate a fair and reasonable chance of success.

Many readers will have seen or taken part in a hurdle race, and they will know that all the hurdles are set at the same height. An objective test is a kind of hurdle race, but one in which each hurdle (or item) is set at a slightly different height from the others, the height of the hurdle being the degree of difficulty of an item. If one could set a test in which each succeeding item was a little more difficult than the last for every candidate, and in which the instructions stated that as soon as a candidate knocked down a hurdle (i.e. failed to answer an item) he had to stop, a distribution of marks would be obtained which directly reflected each candidate's performance on that test in relation to the performance of all the other candidates. The construction of such a test is, however, clearly impossible: what is difficult for one individual may, for a variety of reasons, be easy for another. It is for this reason that all candidates in an objective test are usually instructed to attempt all the items, and the degree of difficulty of each item is the degree of difficulty not for a single individual but for a representative sample group. It is thus not unfair to the better candidate to award only one mark per item, however difficult the item may be, since performance on the test as a whole should distinguish the good from the less good.

It is perfectly true that the difficulty of an item can be emphasised, and the candidate answering it correctly be rewarded, by giving such an item greater weight, that is to say, by awarding it more marks than are awarded for other items. Apart from the fact that such weighting will complicate the scoring procedures, research in the United States—for example by Guilford and Phillips—suggests that neither the validity nor the reliability of the test as a whole is improved by weighting in this way. The balance of the test is certainly altered by weighting, but it is doubtful whether its quality is improved. If one area of the content to be covered is regarded as being twice as important as another, it is better to set twice as many items upon it than to weight the scoring of a similar number for each area in the proportion 2 to 1. Moreover, the suggestion that certain items deserve greater mark weighting than others because of their complexity or because of the time needed to read them can often be met by reconstructing them so that the material used yields more than one item, all of which can be independently scored.

There is one important point that should be mentioned about the hurdle analogy, which illustrates the dangers of all comparisons of this kind. We have talked of a 'hurdle race', and this implies speed. The majority of objective tests, however, are not speed tests: they are timed in such a way that over 90 per cent of the candidates taking them can finish the paper. This is particularly true of subject achievement tests. Such tests are instead 'power tests', tests designed to identify those candidates who have the most knowledge.

In an earlier paragraph one of the possible advantages of an objective test was mentioned and this raises an important question that concerns both the candidate and the teacher: namely, what are the advantages and disadvantages of an objective test, or, to put it perhaps in a more positive way, what are its strengths and weaknesses? These are summarised below.

Strengths

1   An objective test can pose a whole series of precise problems which can be clearly stated and quickly answered.
2   An objective test can provide a wide content coverage. Moreover, because of the comparative precision of each item, the danger of overlap is reduced. The number of items also reduces the possibility of question spotting.
3   An objective test can be speedily and accurately marked.
4   An objective test can be tried out in advance (pre-tested), and on the basis of the evidence obtained tests of differing levels of difficulty can be constructed.

Weaknesses

1 An objective test cannot test written expression or a candidate's ability to develop an argument.
2 An objective test can all too easily test only factual recall or simple understanding of facts.
3 An objective test may encourage candidates to guess the answers to questions.
4 An objective test is difficult and expensive to construct.

In listing these points no attempt has been made to compare objective tests with other types of test (for example, essay, practical, oral). To do so is an unrewarding exercise except in relation to a particular subject at a particular level. What ought to be done instead is to consider what one is trying to test and then to look at the best possible way of doing it, taking advantage of the strengths of particular approaches and being aware of the weaknesses. It follows from this that objective tests will be more appropriate for some subjects than for others, and that within subjects certain aspects will be more appropriately tested by objective items than by any other method.

Neither in the list of strengths and weaknesses nor in the chapter as a whole has any direct reference been made to the two most important technical concepts in testing—reliability and validity. Aspects of both have been referred to, but this is not enough; reliability and validity need to be considered more carefully. When we talk of the *reliability* of a test, we mean the consistency with which a set of test scores measures whatever it dose measure; and when we talk of *validity*, we mean the accuracy with which a set of test scores measures what it sets out to measure. The difference is contained in the contrast between the words 'consistency' and 'accuracy'.

There are three major factors which contribute to the reliability of a test: the first is the extent to which different forms of the same test are comparable—for example, the papers set by an examining board in successive years in the same subject; the second is the consistency with which those who take the test perform upon it; the third is the consistency with which the test is marked. Translated into human terms these three factors are: those who draw up the specifications of the test and construct it, the candidate who takes the test, and the marker. It has already been suggested that among the strengths of objective tests are their ability to pose precise problems and the consistency with which they can be marked. Both these points will be emphasised in more detail later in the book. It would, therefore, seem reasonable to suggest that in relation to the first and third factors (the comparability of two test forms and the consistency of marking), objective tests are likely to achieve high reliability. The reliability of any test can be calculated and defined, but the design of an objective test and the precision with which it is constructed make it likely not only that it will be more reliable than other types of test but that its reliability will be easier to define. Reliability should not, however, be equated with excellence. If the test itself does not test things which are worth while, the fact that it tests them reliably will not make it a good test.

As far as the second variable (the candidate) is concerned, no testing technique or format can ensure reliability here. All one can say, perhaps, is that where the use of differing techniques makes different demands upon a candidate, the objective test may well prove more reliable, in that it ensures that the candidate who has noticeable strengths and weaknesses does have a chance of providing a variety of evidence about himself. As one of a number of means of asking the candidates to provide such evidence, objective testing can here, too, make an important contribution to the overall reliability of tests.

Although the reliability of a test can be calculated, it is extremely difficult in any accurate sense to measure a test's validity. To form any estimate of validity, it is necessary to study the test itself and, wherever possible, the objectives that have formed, as it were, the basis of the test construction brief and the specifications that were drawn up for the test. Such a study is necessary, whether it is intended to try to determine the validity of the test directly by critical analysis or indirectly by an analysis of its correlations with some valid external criteria such as teachers' estimates.

Validity is essentially a matter of degree. There is no such thing as an absolutely valid or an absolutely invalid test; there are simply more or less valid tests. The validity of any test depends not only upon its reliability and relevance, but also upon the purpose for which it is to be used and the skill with which it is used to achieve this purpose. Finally, the validity of any test depends upon the particular group taking it, a group, which, it is hoped, those responsible for constructing the test will have had carefully in mind throughout its preparation.

In its construction an objective test, as will be seen later, requires the careful consideration of objectives and the drawing up of specifications. It also involves a group of people rather than a single individual; in addition, the various stages in its development are carefully planned. It is not unreasonable, therefore, to hope that such a test will achieve a higher validity than a test which is less carefully constructed—a description which would not be unfair to many of the assessment procedures in common use today both inside and outside the classroom.

In the setting out of the strengths and weaknesses of objective tests the major emphasis has been placed upon those used in secondary school external testing, and little or nothing has been said about the value of objective tests for internal educational guidance. To criticise such an omission is reasonable, since this aspect is important; but it should be emphasised that our main concern here is the limited one of discussing objective testing as a method which it is considered can make a valuable contribution to valid and reliable assessment at the secondary level. In attempting to achieve this, the teacher can play as important a part in the classroom as can the examining body outside it, but both need to have some knowledge of the techniques involved. Such knowledge is equally needed if the objective test is to be used for diagnosis rather than assessment, and the fact that the emphasis of the book is slanted in a particular direction does not mean that we undervalue any of the uses that can be made of objective tests or, indeed, of tests as a whole.

In the United Kingdom teachers and others involved in education are naturally very concerned about the effect that particular types of test questions may have upon teaching practice. This matter of the 'backwash effect', as it is called, is obviously one which has to be given careful thought when objective tests are considered. One important reason for this concern is that it has become too much a habit in this country to look upon test results as the sole piece of evidence upon which to judge a candidate's suitability for higher education or for certain kinds of employment. In consequence, teachers regard it as very important that their pupils are given as good a chance as possible of passing whatever test or tests it is necessary for them to pass; and this will inevitably mean study of, and practice upon, the type of question set in these tests.

One way of relieving this backwash effect is to use a number of different techniques within a single test—in other words, to make the test a 'composite'. This is in agreement with a point stressed earlier, namely, that we should make the best possible use of the strengths of any particular technique. Candidates may therefore expect to see not completely objective tests, but tests of which one section is objective. For example, an O level history test may have 40 per cent of its marks awarded to an objective section and 60 per cent awarded to essay questions. This kind of approach will not be confined to objective items and essay questions, but will extend to orals, practicals and internal assessment. Tests will almost certainly become increasingly a mixture, a mixture designed not to confuse candidates and to discover what they do not know, but to enable them to display their knowledge to the best advantage and to encourage the teacher to teach the subject, confident in the knowledge that if he does so adequately the test will fairly reflect his pupils' relative abilities in that subject. If this aim is realised, those who use tests to select are likely to obtain information which will be more useful to them than the information they receive at present.

It is worth considering—even if the consideration must inevitably be both selective and superficial—the effects which the development and more general use of objective tests in the United Kingdom are likely to have upon the three groups who will be most immediately concerned: the candidates who will take the tests; the teachers who will teach the candidates and will have the opportunity to use objective tests in the classroom and perhaps take part in their construction; and, finally, the staff of the organisations which may develop tests for use in external assessment.

The candidates will need to become familiar with a new type of test, and three main differences will be immediately apparent to them. First, they will be required to read and think rather than to think and write. Secondly, in order to answer the questions it will only be necessary for them to make a series of marks on the answer sheet or booklet in accordance with a detailed set of instructions. Thirdly, instead of answering some ten questions they will be asked to answer as many as sixty or seventy separate items in a comparatively short time.

The teacher and, it is stressed, we are concerned chiefly with the teacher in the secondary school—in addition to learning about the procedure and problems involved in the development and construction of objective tests, will also become aware of and take part in the discussion of issues which will be raised by their use, for example, the backwash effect already mentioned and the effect of guessing.

The staff of the organisations involved in the development of testing for external use will need to become more professional in their approach. In saying this, it is not suggested that other testing techniques do not require such an approach, or that the examining boards have not been professional hitherto. Objective tests, however, by their mode of construction, by the need for absolute precision in their wording, by reason of the number of items involved and by the opportunities they provide for statistical treatment both before and after use, compel a more professional approach than has perhaps been necessary in the past. Bodies who construct external tests ought no longer even to consider setting tests without the help of the statistician, the educational psychologist and the psychometrician.

CHAPTER 2

Types of objective item

There are a considerable number of forms that can be taken by objective items; for example, Gerberich's (1956)* *Specimen Objective Test Items* lists about a dozen. In this chapter we shall not attempt to list all the types, but shall concentrate on a few of the more important. Indeed, reference to published tests will show that in practice comparatively few varieties are used. Before we discuss item types, it is important to mention that there is a distinction between the short-answer item, which may be semi-objective in form, and the fully objective item as defined in the opening chapter. In the short-answer item the candidate is required to *supply* the answer; in the objective item proper he is asked to *select* it. This represents a fundamental difference, not only in the mechanics of construction but also in the processes required of the candidate to provide the answer.

Short-answer items

The short-answer item is commonly used in classroom tests in the United Kingdom. It is not so objective that tests consisting of such items could be marked by clerks working solely from a key, or by such machines as are at present available for marking objective tests. The phrase 'as are at present available' has been used deliberately, since new developments in machine scoring, notably by Professor E. F. Lindquist at the Measurement Research Center in Iowa City in the United States, may shortly make it possible for a machine to mark a wide range of pre-selected responses as 'correct'. This, while it is not free response, is certainly freer response than is possible at present if mechanical marking is used.

* Bibliographical details are given on p. 109 ff.

The short-answer item has a number of varieties, for example, the question: 'Who succeeded James I as King of England?' ....; the association: 'Opposite each city write the country of which it is the capital: Paris, London, etc., ...; and the completion: 'The name of the author of the novel *Pride and Prejudice* is ....'. All the illustrations here are, of course, purely factual and only admit of one correct answer. Thus they are completely objective, and the criticism of this item type mentioned above does not apply. However, the answer to the 'completion' variety, the one most commonly used in the United Kingdom, need not be confined to one word; it can consist of several lines or a paragraph, and this may require a candidate to apply his knowledge rather than merely to repeat it. Such short-answer items are very frequently used by the classroom teacher, and Nuffield Science examinations have shown how the completion variety can be used with value in a public examination. They have also been used in a number of CSE examinations, particularly in mathematics and history. An example of this kind of question, as used in a Nuffield Physics paper,* is as follows:

'A book on space flight contains the picture opposite and states that the satellite may follow one of three kinds of path according to its "launch velocity". Write a few sentences in exposition of this.' The examination booklet, which is the answer booklet, provides some five lines for the answer.

It should be emphasised that the short-answer item is not nearly as easy to construct as it may appear to be at first sight, as the attempt to overcome the main problem—that of ambiguity—is liable to result in the question becoming so specific as to lead the candidates directly to the answer. In setting short-answer items it is important to ensure that the information which they provide about the candidate cannot be obtained more satisfactorily by means of a properly constructed objective item or by an essay. If this point is not borne in mind,

* Reproduced by permission of the Oxford and Cambridge Schools Examination Board.

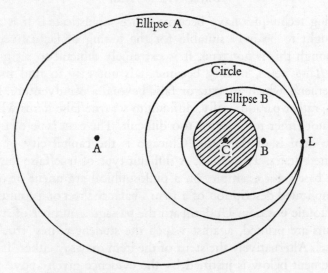

Notes: C is the centre of the Earth,
   L is launch point, about 6,000 miles above Earth in this diagram,
   A is one focus of ellipse A, and B is one focus of ellipse B.

test constructors may well lose the advantage of objectivity in marking, while not obtaining the kind of information that can be provided by a more extended piece of writing.

Objective items

As mentioned earlier, published tests contain a comparatively small number of varieties of the choice or selection form of item—the objective item proper—and this chapter will deal only with those which are most commonly used: the true/false or yes/no, the matching, the multiple-choice and the multiple-completion, which is merely a more elaborate form of multiple-choice.

TRUE/FALSE ITEMS

The true/false item has always been regarded with suspicion by opponents of objective testing on the grounds that it is particularly susceptible to guessing, a problem which will be discussed in more detail in chapter 5. Indeed, it would probably be true to say that it has been less frequently used in recent years as testing techniques have become more sophisticated. It is also thought to be only suitable for the testing of factual recall, although this is not true. It is extremely difficult to set good true/false items, mainly because it is not easy to find many statements which are true or false beyond a peradventure. It is also, rather paradoxically, difficult to set true/false items which are not either too easy or too difficult. The easy type of true/false item is of the type 'Chicago is the capital city of the United States. True/false'. A difficult type of true/false item is one based, for example, on a philosophical argument or on a complicated description of a firm's balance sheet or a country's economic position. Underneath the passage a number of statements are printed, against which the student writes 'true' or 'false'. Alternatively the stem of the item may say either 'If the statement below is justified by the evidence given above, say yes', or 'If the statement below is not justified by the evidence given above, say no'. Such an item can be extremely difficult to answer, although it may be argued that what is really being tested is verbal comprehension and that this could be better tested in a different way. A quite complex form of true/false item, which is useful in science subjects, is one in which the student indicates whether a statement is false or whether one of a set of qualifications is necessary to make the statement true.

Directions

Each of the following items may be true without qualification, true with qualification, or false. If it is true without qualification, circle the T and mark a 3 in the space provided. If it is true with one of the listed qualifications, circle T and mark the number of the appropriate qualification in the space. If the item is false, circle the F.

Statements	*Qualifications*
T F .... The total resistance in an electrical circuit is equal to the sum of the individual resistances.	1 if the resistances are connected in parallel.

Statements	Qualifications
T F .... The total current in an electrical circuit is equal to the sum of the currents in the individual parts of the of the circuit.	2 if the resistances are connected in series. 3 no qualification.
T F .... The total current in an electrical circuit is equal to the electromotive force in the circuit divided by the resistance of the circuit.	
T F .... The power supplied to a circuit is equal to the product of the total resistance and the amount of current in the circuit.	

There are also a number of variants of the true/false item which can be usefully included in tests in which the absolute truth or falsity of the statement or fact is replaced by a number of possibilities. If, for example, we wanted to find out whether candidates knew the doctrines and practices of the Pharisees and Sadducees, we could list a number of statements and ask the candidates to write against them the letter A if it was true of the Pharisees, B if it was true of the Sadducees, C if it was true of both, and D if it was true of neither.

Another variant of this type is where two statements are made, separated by the word 'because'. Candidates are asked to look at these statements and answer them in the light of a key which reads:

A   both statements are true and are correctly related to each other

B   both statements are true but are not correctly related to each other

C   the first statement is true but the second statement is not true

D   neither statement is true.

Several items can be based on this key if required. The main problem in such an item lies in finding statements other than of a purely factual character which are true or false in absolute terms, and it is therefore liable to test trivia.

In effect what is being done in many of these examples is to construct a basically true/false item in a multiple-choice form, repeating the same four choices for each statement or argument. Indeed, many experienced test constructors would say that true/false items can almost always be asked more usefully and more reliably in a multiple-choice form, either indirectly as in the above examples or directly where the four options provided are:

A Yes because . . . .
B Yes because . . . .
C No because   . . . .
D No because   . . . .

MATCHING ITEMS

The second of the objective item types to be considered is the 'matching', of which there are two chief variants: first, those which are based on the matching of the contents of one list against the contents of another (these lists may consist of virtually anything, for example, dates, names, songs, phrases, statements, diagrams), and secondly, those based upon the classification of statements. In some books the first variant is referred to as the matching item and the second as the classification item. Examples of both follow.

Matching

On the line in front of each war write the number of the treaty which concluded it.

Treaty		War
1 Paris		
2 Vienna	. . . .	League of Augsburg
3 Versailles	. . . .	Spanish Succession

	Treaty		War
4	Aix La Chapelle	....	Austrian Succession
5	Utrecht	....	American Independence
6	Ryswick		

Classification

This type of item is always based upon a number of pieces of information about which several questions are subsequently asked, for example: 'Items 1 to 3 are based on certain functions of the Bank of England given below:

A it regulates the country's credit
B it acts as lender of last resort
C it acts as the Government's bank
D it co-operates with international financial institutions.

Which of the above functions

1 causes the Bank to conduct open cheque operations?
2 gives the Bank the right to negotiate with the International Monetary Fund?
3 ensures that the Bank of England holds the country's gold reserves?'

The instructions for this would ask the candidates either to block out or write in the appropriate letter for each item, depending on whether a separate answer sheet was used or not.

The simplest type of matching item, such as the one illustrated, is chiefly used for the identification of names, dates, meanings, and similar associations. It will be noted that in the example given some of the treaties do not match with the wars. This is known as imperfect matching; it is much more frequently used than an item which has perfect matching, since when there is a perfect match, the last pair will not function at all as a valid item because the candidates will be able to provide the correct answer by elimination. They will also be able to go a long way towards answering the last but one pair by elimination, and considerable encouragement is thus given to indiscriminate guessing.

As with all objective items, good matching items are not

easy to construct, the most common fault being lack of homogeneity between the lists in the two columns. In general, their role is rather limited, since the answers can in effect be no more than a word or a short phrase, and they thus tend to be concerned with purely factual information and place a premium on recall. The classification type, as the illustration shows, is likely to be rather more useful, since it is very suitable for dealing with topics which require explanation and criticism, and can thus test a rather higher level of learning.

A hybrid version which is part matching and part classification is as follows:

'Questions 1 to 6 are based on the Parliamentary Reform Acts of
A   1832
B   1867
C   1884
D   1918
E   1928
Against each statement given below write the letter of the Reform Act to which it refers. [If a separate mark sheet was being used, different instructions would be given.]

1   Women over the age of 30 obtained the vote.
2   The size of the electorate increased from 435,000 to 652,000.
3   The holder of copyhold land value £10 p.a. obtained the vote.
4   Boroughs with a population of less than 10,000 lost one of their two M.P.s.
5   The borough franchise was equated with the country franchise.
6   All males over the age of 21 obtained the vote.'

This item, while it does not attempt to test any of the higher abilities, provides a quick and reliable way of asking for the kind of information that is rewarded in questions that appear at present in many of our existing tests, such as 'Outline the steps by which universal suffrage was obtained in Britain in the 19th and 20th centuries'. As with the true/false items, it is possible to write matching and classification items in a multiple-choice form. The Parliamentary Reform item above, for example, could be re-written as follows:

> Questions 1–4 (or whatever the numbers are) refer to the following Parliamentary Reform Acts:
>
> 1 1832
> 2 1867
> 3 1884
> 4 1918
> 5 1928
>
> 1 Which Act gave the vote to women over 30?
>   A 5
>   B 2
>   C 3
>   D 4
>
> 2 Which Act increased the size of the electorate from 435,000 to 652,000?
>   A 1
>   B 3
>   C 2
>   D 4

And so on.

MULTIPLE-CHOICE ITEMS

The third type of objective item to be considered is the multiple-choice. Here the item consists of a stem in the form of an introductory question or an incomplete statement, together with a number of responses or options of which one is correct and the remainder, usually called distractors, are incorrect. The multiple-choice item asks the candidate to identify the response which is correct for the particular question asked. Each item normally stands on its own without the necessity of being related in any way to any other item, so that on the one hand it avoids the problem of absolute truth or absolute falsity, which creates difficulties for the true/false item, and on the other it avoids the necessity of finding relationships, which creates difficulties for the matching item. Moreover, by being completely objective in form it avoids the problem of subjectivity in marking which bedevils both the essay and the short-answer question.

The multiple-choice item is by far the most widely used objective item in current tests and can be adapted to a wide variety of approaches using additional materials such as graphs, cartoons, maps and written material. A number of examples of multiple-choice items in history and physics are given below, the correct response being underlined in each case. All the items are phrased positively except for no. 4, which is phrased in negative form. The question of the suitability or unsuitability of negative items is considered later, and this should be regarded merely as an example.

Items 1 and 2 refer to the cartoon* shown opposite.

1   In what year was this cartoon most likely to have been drawn?
    A   1885
    B   1894
    C   1903
    D   1910

2   Balfour was unable to go as fast as Chamberlain because
    A   he belonged to a different political party
    B   he feared that he would split his party by doing so
    C   he held a less important post in the Government
    D   he believed the monarch disapproved of the proposed policy.

3   The doubling of the population of the United States between 1789 and 1815 was due primarily to
    A   the importing of slaves
    B   natural increase via the birth rate
    C   European immigration
    D   a decline in the death rate.

* Reproduced by permission of Punch.

HISTORY REVERSES ITSELF.

PAPA JOSEPH TAKING MASTER ARTHUR A PROTECTION WALK.

PAPA JOSEPH. 'COME ALONG, MASTER ARTHUR, DO STEP OUT.'
MASTER ARTHUR. 'THAT'S ALL VERY WELL, BUT YOU KNOW I CANNOT GO
AS FAST AS YOU DO.'

4 Which of the following statements about the Act of Union
between Britain and Ireland in 1800 is <u>NOT</u> true?

A It allowed Roman Catholics to become members of
the Westminster Parliament

B It completed the parliamentary union of the United
Kingdom

C It increased the elected element in the House of Lords
at Westminster

D It marked the end of an independent parliament for the
whole of Ireland

5 An electric cell of e.m.f. 2 volt is connected to an ammeter

of resistance 5 ohm. It is found that the ammeter reads 1/3 ampere. The internal resistance of the cell is

A   0·1 ohm
B   1·0 ohm
C   1·2 ohm
D   5/3 ohm
E   3/5 ohm.

6   An object is placed at a distance of 10 cm from the surface of a convex mirror of radius of curvature 20 cm. The image formed in the mirror is

A   real and erect
B   real and inverted
C   virtual and erect
D   virtual and inverted
E   virtual and at infinity.

7   When a magnetised steel needle is heated in a flame it loses its magnetism. This is because

A   the electrons in the atoms are speeded up
B   the needle expands and the magnetic poles are further apart
C   the lines of force in the magnetised needle are absorbed in the flame
D   the 'molecular' magnets cease to be magnets
E   the 'molecular' magnets cease to be aligned.

Items 8 to 11 are based on verbal stimulus material. They are only used as an example, and it should be noted that they are intended to find out attitudes and that there is not necessarily a correct answer.

Mr and Mrs Brown are elderly, house-bound and childless. They live in a cul-de-sac which is to be turned into a children's play-road and barred to traffic. They protest strongly to the local council about the use to which the road is to be put. Their main objections, which are well known to their neighbours, are:

1   they are entitled to peace and quiet in their old age

2   the vans that deliver their essential food supplies will no
    longer be able to deliver to their door.

8   What should the local council do?
    A   Abandon the project of the play-road
    B   Re-house Mr and Mrs Brown in another street
    C   Accept responsibility for the delivery of the food
    D   Remove the Browns' tax liability as compensation
    E   Ask the children to be quiet when they use the play-
        road

9   What should the local children do?
    A   Ignore the old people completely
    B   Torment the Browns for being spoil-sports
    C   Refuse to use the play-road in deference to the Browns
    D   Offer to help deliver the foodstuffs to the Browns
    E   Use the play-road at certain times of the day only

10 What should the Browns do if the play-road is put into
    operation?
    A   Appeal to the Government to have the project stopped
    B   Sue the local council for loss of amenities
    C   Move to a house in another road
    D   Seek police protection from disturbance caused by
        children
    E   Accept the majority decision of the council despite the
        inconvenience of the play-road

11 What should the other residents of the cul-de-sac do?
    A   Join the Browns in their protest, even though the play-
        road is urgently needed
    B   Offer to help the Browns by delivering their food
        supplies
    C   Supervise the children's behaviour in the play-road
    D   Help the Browns to move to another road
    E   Ignore the Browns and encourage their children to use
        the play-road as they see fit

Where additional written material or pictures, maps and diagrams are used, item writers must ensure that the questions asked could not equally well have been asked without any reference to the material. One should also avoid turning the item into a verbal comprehension test by asking questions which are based primarily on the ability to understand the passage instead of ones which get at the understanding or abilities in the subject actually being tested. The following three items, based on a passage describing the Dred Scott Decision, could equally well have been asked on their own. The passage, beyond providing a more extended illustration, contributes nothing to the item.

'Slavery

The Dred Scott Decision, meaning that the territories had no choice but to accept slavery, was a blow to "popular sovereignty"; but Douglas had stuck to his doctrine courageously and defied Buchanan and the Southern Democrats when they had attempted to impose the Lecompton Constitution on Kansas. In the debate, Lincoln placed Douglas in a dilemma by asking whether the people of a territory could, in any lawful way, exclude slavery from their limits. Apparently, Douglas must either accept the Dred Scott Decision and admit popular sovereignty to be a farce, or separate from his party by repudiating a dictum of the Supreme Court.'

1 The doctrine of popular sovereignty was first invoked in the United States at the time of the
   A Missouri Compromise
   B Compromise of 1850
   C Kansas-Nebraska Bill
   D Wade-Davis Manifesto.

2 The Lecompton Constitution was framed by
   A a convention of pro-slavery Kansans
   B a convention of anti-slavery Kansans
   C President James Buchanan
   D John C. Calhoun.

3   The Lincoln-Douglas Debates were conducted in
    A   Missouri
    B   Kansas
    C   Nebraska
    D   Illinois.

Wherever possible, more than one item should be written when using stimulus material, since this provides a greater return for the extra reading time that will be required.

While the multiple-choice item can and often is used to measure insignificant and superficial knowledge, it can also, if properly constructed, be used effectively to measure more complex abilities such as analysis, as is shown in *Multiple-Choice Questions: A Close Look* (Educational Testing Service 1963). The next chapter will deal in more detail with problems of item writing, but there is one important problem that requires discussion here, and that concerns the number of options that it is desirable to have in a multiple-choice item. Most current tests favour items with either four or five options. The main argument in favour of five is that it reduces the possibility of guessing or, put in another way, lengthens the odds against a random guess being successful. The main argument against five and in favour of four is that it is extremely difficult, particularly in the social sciences and humanities, to find five good options for most items. This can result in one of the distractors being virtually inoperative, since it is obviously wrong, or because it is similar to another response as a result of hair splitting in an attempt to find an extra option. In these circumstances what in reality has been set is a four-option item, and it is surely sensible, therefore, to start looking for four good options as the basis upon which the items are to be written rather than to attempt to find a fifth which does not contribute anything.

MULTIPLE-COMPLETION ITEMS

The final objective item type to be considered in this chapter is the multiple-completion. This is merely a variety of multiple-choice, but since it is rather different in construction it is worth considering as a separate type. The item is set in two-tier form,

O.T.—3

the first tier consisting of a number of responses, one or more of which may be correct. The second tier consists of a series of numbers which provide different combinations of possible correct responses. This second tier actually forms the options upon which the candidate is required to make a decision. Two examples follow:

1 Which of the following contributed to the Liberal victory in the United Kingdom election of 1906?
   I   Nonconformist irritation at alterations to the licensing laws
   II The employment of Chinese labour in the South African mines
   III Working class irritation at the Taff Vale decision
   IV Joseph Chamberlain's Tariff Reform campaign
   A   IV only
   B   I and II only
   C   I, III and IV only
   D   I, II, III and IV.

2 If you were conducting research upon a social problem, in which order would you carry out the following steps?
   I   Seeking the evidence
   II Formulating the hypotheses
   III Preparing the solution
   IV Analysing the evidence
   V   Defining the problem
   A   II, V, IV, I, III
   B   V, II, I, IV, III
   C   IV, V, I, III, II
   D   I, IV, II, V, III
   E   V, I, II, IV, III

This item format has a number of advantages; it enables a multiple-choice format to be used for an item which has more than one correct response, and it compels the candidate to consider every piece of information given in the item and then to come to a decision which may involve both judgement and selection. It thus tests more than factual knowledge. The candidate who knows the facts will, of course, answer the item correctly, but not until he has had to review the possibilities and satisfy himself on their suitability or unsuitability. This item format has also the mechanical advantage that four options can be produced from only three statements.

The multiple-completion item is, however, not without its disadvantages. It is open to criticism on the grounds that it involves a considerable amount of reading for small reward and that this places a premium on verbal comprehension. It has also been suggested that its somewhat complicated format may confuse candidates, although this problem can be largely overcome by ensuring that the candidates are provided with clear instructions and have the opportunity to practise answering sample items. For the test constructor, too, the multiple-completion items cause problems, and great care must be taken to ensure that the answer is not given away to the candidate.

At present, when comparatively little use has been made of objective tests in the United Kingdom, the relative advantages and disadvantages of the multiple-completion item have not been adequately assessed, and it would seem reasonable for a number of these items to be tried out in tests in order to obtain evidence of their value.

The reader will have realised that certain item types are likely to be more appropriate to testing certain abilities and skills than others. It is suggested that in history the following might be tested: knowledge and understanding of facts; the perceiving of relationships, for example, cause and effect; and the ability to interpret verbal and non-verbal material. In physics one might wish to test: the knowledge of facts, definitions and laws; the understanding of physical phenomena; the appreciation of experimental method and the evaluation of observations; the application of physical principles to unfamiliar situations. Within the boundaries of the cognitive domain for both these subjects, a test could be constructed using multiple-choice and multiple-completion items only. The number of different item types used will, of course, vary according to what it is wished to test in a subject area.

CHAPTER 3

Constructing the test

At present the majority of public tests in the United Kingdom consist of questions which the candidate is required to answer by means of a piece or pieces of continuous writing. While the basic details and terminology used in the procedures for setting papers vary slightly from examining board to examining board, the basic outlines remain much the same. All the question papers are set by chief examiners; they are then scrutinised by a moderator, who comments on such matters as ambiguity of wording, the balance of the question paper and its relation to the syllabus. When appropriate—for example, in mathematics—the question paper is later closely scrutinised by an assessor, who actually works the paper in order to ensure that the questions asked can be solved in the time allowed. All the comments made during these procedures are then considered by a standing advisory committee, composed in the main of practising teachers in the subject concerned; it is the responsibility of this committee to approve the final version of the paper.

Objective tests will require a different approach. The construction of a test containing objective items, whether these constitute the whole of the test or only a part, will be undertaken by several people, who will work together as a team. Under ideal conditions these people would be divided into two groups:

1 subject experts, who will almost always be practising teachers at some level in the subject concerned;
2 measurement experts, who will normally have a qualification in psychometrics or educational measurement.

The role which each should play in the construction of the final test will be made clear when the procedures are described later. It is essential, however, to emphasise that objective test construction is a co-operative venture shared between all those who take part in the work. The subject expert, on the one hand, must not think that a valid objective test or item can be constructed and tried out without some expert advice, nor, on the other hand, must the measurement expert make test construction into a mystique in which the ordinary teacher cannot participate without lengthy special training.

The stages in the construction of an objective test are set out below. For the purposes of illustration we will assume that the test is a GCE Ordinary level paper on British history, covering the period 1789–1867 and lasting one hour. We will also assume that it is a test which is being developed for external use on a sizable scale, though, as will be suggested later, the procedures can be carried out by classroom teachers who have in mind a more limited use of the test.

1 Drawing up the specifications for the test.
2 Allotting the item writing.
3 Writing the items.
4 Editing the items.
5 Assembling the test forms for pre-testing.
6 Organising the pre-test.
7 Analysing the results of the pre-test.
8 Assembling the final version of the test.

In order to implement this outline, a committee will have to be established; this will be called the specification committee. It will probably comprise about ten members, but this will depend on the amount of item writing and editing which the members themselves intend to undertake. (This point will be returned to later in the chapter.) The great majority of these members will be subject experts, people who are selected first and foremost for their knowledge of the subject under consideration (in this case history) and its teaching at the level appropriate to the test in question (in this case O level). Experience in writing objective items will also be valuable, although it is not essential. The committee should also have at least one member who has experience of editing tests and who is capable of ensuring that the stages in the construction of the test are carried out thoroughly and in logical sequence. This person ought, whenever possible, to be a member of the professional staff of the organisation responsible for developing and using the test, and ought to act as secretary to the committee.

Finally, it is highly desirable that the committee has a member who is professionally qualified in measurement theory and who has had considerable experience in the mechanics of test construction in general. Ideally, such a person should be a permanent member of the committee and should attend all its meetings, since the best tests emerge from a constant interaction of the subject and measurement experts. This, however, may not be possible, since at present qualified people in this field are few and far between. In these circumstances the best alternative would be to have available such an expert on a consultancy basis; this would ensure that errors in construction are detected and eliminated, although it would prevent the continuous discussion of problems which is so valuable.

Readers may already be saying that the proposed procedure is all very well for a large professional organisation with a qualified staff and with money, but what is its use for the teacher who wants to construct a test for his or her class? The answer to this question must be that the careful preparation of any test, at whatever level it may be used, is of vital importance. Although teachers primarily concerned with classroom testing may find it better to use more traditional methods of assessment, it is important that they should not only be aware of different types of test and their preparation, but that they should actually put this knowledge into practice. In order to do this with objective tests they could with advantage, in co-operation with their colleagues and with advice from any suitable source, try to develop tests on the lines suggested in this book. As experience grows in this type of testing so the number of individuals with experience will increase and the problems ease. A bad test, however, can do nothing but harm, whatever its level.

The first task for our committee is to draw up the specifications for the test, and this again is an exercise which the classroom teacher can carry out with advantage. In drawing up the specification it is necessary to consider (a) the content to be covered; (b) the number of items to be used; (c) the skills or abilities to be tested. In this context an objective test on its own is being considered, although in practice the objective component is likely to form but a part of the total test, for example, one hour out of two and a half hours in history at Ordinary level. If this is so, the specification committee will have to ensure that the test as a whole is a fully integrated single test and not several tests. They will also have to decide whether they wish the objective section to cover a part of the syllabus or to range widely over the whole, as it would do if it formed the complete test.

The answer to the first point to be considered in the specification (that is, the content) may be provided by the syllabus and question paper of an existing examination. In our example of British history at O level, 1789–1867, it may well be that a syllabus already exists and can provide some guidance. Outline syllabuses in history tend to be very brief, and need to be considered in conjunction with past question papers in order to give an idea of the balance of the examination. But even scrutiny of these question papers will not provide the kind of detailed information that is needed for the construction of an objective test. It must be borne in mind that such a test will consist of between fifty and one hundred items, so that the content area can be covered in much greater detail than it can in an essay test. The specification must, therefore, be detailed; this means that the committee must go back to first principles, taking the two end dates 1789 and 1867 and deciding what they consider ought to be covered within these dates. In the United States the first step in the construction of most achievement tests is to define a series of general objectives for the subject concerned. This approach results in large measure from the fact that such tests in the United States are not normally syllabus-based, although constant use of specific textbooks may in the long run produce the same effect as a prescribed syllabus. In the United Kingdom we normally have a syllabus for a public examination, even if a very broadly defined one. Considerations, therefore, of the limits of

the syllabus and the kind of abilities that we wish the candidate
to demonstrate and which it is considered desirable to test, should
provide a specific framework for test construction without the
need for a statement of more general objectives. It is, nevertheless, worth emphasising that a consideration of objectives,
whether at the general or the specific level, is all too often neglected. (See chapter 7 for a fuller discussion of this problem.)

The content of the test under consideration can be looked
at in a number of ways—for example, chronologically or by
subject matter—and it will be necessary to devise a grid which
takes account of the way in which the committee wish the
subject matter to be divided in order to obtain a proper balance.
For example, they might on this occasion wish to see equal
weighting given to the three periods, 1789–1815, 1816–1846,
1847–1867; or they might, on the other hand, regard one of the
three periods as more important than the others. They might
then consider the division as being between questions in the
following subject matter areas: domestic/political; social and
economic; foreign affairs. The extent to which this division is
carried out is a matter for the committee to decide, and will
obviously differ in history from period to period and according
to the level of the examination. Decisions on such matters will
inevitably depend on the number of items envisaged for the
test, its scope and its duration (in this case one hour). We will
assume that on this occasion the committee plans a test of sixty
items, bearing in mind that when the examination is pre-tested
at a later stage the time allocation in relation to the number
of items can be assessed with a high degree of accuracy. On the
basis of a sixty-item test the following decisions are taken:

Chronological division	No. of items	Content division	No. of items
1789–1815	20	Domestic/political	24
1816–1846	20	Social and economic	15
1847–1867	20	Foreign affairs (including Empire)	21
Overlapping items up to a maximum of	10	Overlapping items up to a maximum of	10

It is very likely that certain of the questions will overlap either in the chronological divisions or in the content areas, and this has been allowed for by indicating the maximum number of items, out of the total of sixty, which it is considered should overlap boundaries.

The third aspect of the specification to be considered relates to the abilities or skills that are to be tested. In traditional essay examinations each question can and actually does test a number of different abilities—for example, knowledge of facts, accurate application of facts, comprehension and the exercise of judgement. Rarely is any attempt made to distinguish in detail between these skills in the marks that are finally awarded, although the candidate who shows that he can exercise judgement and analyse material will almost always secure better marks than the candidate who merely knows the basic facts. In an objective test, however, the number of items permits one to devise questions which specifically attempt to measure a particular skill or ability. The ability which it is proposed to test will also, of course, be linked closely with the topic of the item. Some topics, for example, lend themselves to a more analytical approach than others. Here again it is important to make the point that the number of items in an objective test can permit the isolation of both topic and ability in a way which is not possible in an essay test.

Professor Bloom of Chicago and a number of his associates have devised a detailed taxonomy of abilities in the cognitive domain. This classification is invaluable as an exercise in critical definition, as a stimulus to thought about educational problems, and as a source of ideas for the teacher. It may, however, be too detailed for use in constructing the particular test paper the committee has in mind. A less detailed classification might be more appropriate, although even here some overlap is inevitable. We will assume that the committee decide to define the abilities they wish to test and the emphasis they wish to place upon them in this way:

1 understanding and recall of facts 30
2 perception of relationships, for example, cause and effect 15
3 interpretation of verbal and non-verbal materials 15

It is not, of course, suggested that exactly this division of emphasis is desirable in every case.

Having taken these decisions, the committee is in a position to draw up a grid, which will form the overall specification for the test. Here again it is worth while for teachers to draw up similar grids, for not only will it enable them to clarify their own thinking, but it will form a clear indication of the number and categories of the items which have to be written. The grid for the test is given below, but it should be stressed that such a grid is intended to provide a general guide and is not to be regarded as something fixed and unalterable.

		A	B	C		X	Y	Z
		Facts	Relation-ships	Inter-pretation	Total	Domestic/ political	Social and economic	Foreign affairs (including Empire)
1	1789–1815	10	5	5	20	6	5	9
2	1816–46	10	5	5	20	9	5	6
3	1847–67	10	5	5	20	9	5	6
Total		30	15	15	60	24	15	21

As a second example, the grid for an O level physics test might be as follows:

	A	B	C		W	X	Y	Z
	Know-ledge	Compre-hension	Applica-tion	Total	Defini-tions, laws and princi-ples	Experi-ments	Explana-tions of physical phenomena	Numerical problems
General physics	8	4	3	15	4	4	4	3
Heat	6	6	3	15	3	5	5	2
Light and sound	8	4	3	15	4	5	4	2
Magnetism and electricity	8	4	3	15	3	5	4	3
Total	30	18	12	60	14	19	17	10

As with the history example, it is assumed that the physics test is to contain sixty items. The physics grid shows that those responsible for designing the test have on this occasion decided that there should be an almost equal distribution of questions on the subject areas; that there should be thirty items on knowledge of facts, eighteen on comprehension and twelve on application. The grid also shows that the test is to contain fourteen items in the field of definitions, laws and principles of physics, nineteen devoted to physical experiments, seventeen to the explanation of physical phenomena, and ten to numerical problems.

In writing items for a test it is necessary to have available at least three times the number of items which it is intended to use. As it has been agreed that the test should have sixty items, arrangements should be made for at least 180 items to be written.

In the rest of this chapter the history grid will be used as the example, and any references to letters or numbers on the grid apply to the history and not to the physics grid.

It may be that members of the specification committee itself will wish to write items, or it may be that all the items will be commissioned from people not on the committee. There is an advantage in having at least some of the items written by members of the specification committee; indeed, to have all the items written by the committee members would ease the administrative problems considerably. What is actually done will obviously vary according to circumstances, but whatever is decided it will mean that between eight and ten item writers will be asked to write twenty to twenty-five items each. These items will be commissioned specifically with reference to the grid; for example, writers will be asked to write so many items from a particular chronological section (1, 2 or 3 on the grid), in a particular subject area (X, Y or Z), and designed to test a particular ability (A, B or C). In addition, the writers will be asked to give their own estimate of the degree of difficulty for each item they write, using the three categories of easy, average and hard. These categories will be related to the candidates for whom the test is being designed, and each writer will be required to write a specified number of items in each category.

The aim will be to cover the complete grid three times. In commissioning the items very specific instructions will be given, not only in regard to the grid but also as to the form in which the items are prepared for the subsequent editing. The various types of items have already been discussed. The item types proposed in any test will be in part linked to the kinds of ability or skill which it is intended to test, since, as we have seen, certain types of item lend themselves to testing one skill rather than others. It is, however, undesirable to have in one test too many different types of item, especially if it is a fairly short test, as this will mean a series of different instructions to the candidate. It has been suggested that for our history test only two item types are necessary: multiple-completion and multiple-choice. In this case the candidate would need only one set of instructions for the test. The number of options for each item has also to be decided, and the arguments for four or for five will need to be considered. In the instructions, examples of the types of items to be used should be set out in correct form as models for the item writers.

At the same time as the item writers receive their instructions, they should also receive a detailed timetable which gives the completion dates for each stage in the preparation of the test.

No example of such instructions or timetable has been included here because there are a variety of possible approaches, and it is essential at this stage in the development of the procedures for objective test construction that flexibility is maintained.

We now come to the actual writing of the items. A study of the chapters on item writing in any publication on the construction of objective tests will reveal that the author can and does do little more than provide a series of basic rules, or do's and don'ts, on item writing together with examples of correct and incorrect items. What is needed to produce a good item, apart from knowing and following these basic rules, is a ready flow of ideas, expertise in the subject concerned, hard work, discussion with fellow workers in the subject field, and willingness to accept constructive criticism. None of these can be provided by a textbook and, furthermore, expertise comes with practice which only the individual can undertake. It should be noted that the basic rules which follow refer by implication to multiple-choice items—although as general points they are obviously applicable to other item types.

1 Avoid ambiguity and irrelevance both in the stem and in the options.
2 Ensure that the problem posed or the question asked is clearly set out in the stem.
3 Ensure that the whole item is as brief as its proper presentation will allow.
4 Ensure that all the options are parallel in construction and content.
5 Ensure that the answer is not given away to the candidate by flaws in the item's wording or construction.
6 Ensure that the intended answer is clearly correct in relation to the question asked, and that the distractors are equally clearly incorrect.

The intention of the first point is obvious. The candidate should not in any way be confused by the wording of the question; he should not have to waste time reading information which is not relevant to the question, or be in any way tricked by it. One important aspect of this last point is whether or not one should state the question in a negative form; e.g. 'Which of the following factors did NOT contribute to Britain's victory in the Seven Years' War?' One school of thought maintains that this should be avoided at all costs, since candidates may easily overlook the negative word; others say that this is perfectly legitimate, as failure to read the item should be penalised, as it is, for example, in an essay test. Our view represents, as it were, a half-way house. Negative items seem to have value on certain occasions, but they should not be used too frequently. Moreover, if they are used, the negative words should be clearly indicated, either by underlining or by capital letters, or preferably both; double negatives should always be avoided.

Another way of putting the second of the rules is that the candidate who knows the answer should be able to give it after reading the stem and before reading the options. If he can do this, the stem must have posed the problem or asked the question with complete clarity.

The third rule may seem obvious, but most people setting tests, particularly if they are teachers, have a great desire to provide instruction in the stem of the item. This should be avoided. Certain problems do, of course, require a more lengthy presentation than others, but wherever a long presentation is necessary, an attempt should be made to write more than one item on the information provided in order to ensure that the candidate gets a reasonable return for the additional work he has had to do.

The fourth rule—that all the options should be parallel—is not so easy to demonstrate, since the definition of 'parallel' will vary from item to item. A rather ridiculous illustration may perhaps bring home the point more clearly, though it should be emphasised that the item is not a good one, breaking, as it does, the rule that the writer should wherever possible ensure that the information required is indicated clearly in the stem. If we say the Battle of Hastings took place in (A) 1066, (B) 1067, (C) 1068, (D) 1069, the options are parallel, since the questioner is interested in the date. If the options are (A) Sussex, (B) Kent, (C) Devon, (D) Dorset, they are still parallel, since the question concerns the county in which the battle took place. If, however, the options are (A) 1066, (B) Sussex, (C) France, (D) bright sunshine, they are clearly not parallel, since each option is presenting a different piece of information about the battle. In editing items for a test, identifying that the options are not parallel and then finding suitable parallel alternatives is far from easy.

Another way in which options can be said to be not parallel is when they are very uneven in length. This unevenness is one of the extraneous clues mentioned in the fifth rule that can give away information to candidates, thus increasing their chances of supplying the correct answer although they do not know why it is correct. Item writers quite often make the correct option the longest because they are determined that it will be beyond doubt correct. If this happens frequently, an alert candidate will note it and when in doubt will select the longest option. Similar clues are afforded where a stem which obviously requires a plural answer is provided with some options in the singular, which can thus be eliminated. Another variation of this is an option or options which clearly do not fit in with the stem. Yet another possible clue is provided when the test constructor places his correct options in a definite sequence. This is not likely to occur when expert advice is available, but it is surprising how often people do follow such set patterns. The sixth point may seem obvious, but it is a frequent cause of faulty items.

The rules, or do's and don'ts, are, like all such rules, somewhat over-simplified; rather more complex problems are involved in item writing than appear at first sight. As the item writer becomes more experienced, he will come to realise that some of the rules are mutually exclusive and that it is possible to write extremely good items which break some of them. Indeed, almost all items represent a compromise between conflicting do's and don'ts and are capable of improvement. Someone somewhere has to say 'Stop! This item does what we want it to do and is perfectly good for our purposes; there is no point in spending more time over it'; or, alternatively, 'This item is not worth the work involved in trying to improve it. Let us move on to the next one.' This is the test editor's job, although at times the chairman of the committee may also need to take this action.

To return to the history test which is being considered here: at this stage it is perhaps as well to remind ourselves that our test is intended to be an external test set by an examining body and as such will be fairly widely taken. Some of the detail given, therefore, may not appear to be immediately applicable to the teacher concerned with the construction of classroom tests. At the same time, the procedures described can be followed without difficulty and with advantage by all people concerned with the construction of tests, whatever their level or whatever the numbers involved. It must, however, be appreciated that test construction is a co-operative venture, and that no one individual can hope to make as much progress as several people working together. The main difference between the teacher and the testing organisation lies in the amount of time which can be devoted to the work and the amount of professional help which is available. Neither of these will affect the basic methods employed, nor will they necessarily produce better tests, although logically they ought to do so.

As we have mentioned, those taking part in the construction of the test will have been given the necessary instructions as well as the detailed timetable for each stage in its production. In drawing up this timetable, the assumption is made that the majority of the test constructors will be practising teachers whose time for this kind of work is limited. The first stage— that is, the drawing up of the specification and the allocation of item writing—should take no more than one or two days if preliminary documentation has been provided and if the item writers have had some experience. A period of three months is not at all unreasonable for writing the items and for any pre- liminary editing that may be decided upon.

The mention of preliminary editing raises the question of the procedure to be adopted for editing the items and, at the risk of a slight digression, this matter is worth considering in some detail. The decision on the procedure to be adopted largely depends upon the availability of expert item writers and editors. Three distinct processes must take place before an item is ready to be used in a pre-test: first, the specification of the test has to be drawn up; secondly, the items have to be written; and thirdly, they have to be edited. These three processes can be carried out by three different groups of people, or one group can involve itself in all three processes. Both approaches have their advantages and disadvantages. In the first case, there would need to be a specification committee, a group of item writers and an editorial committee. In the second case, one committee would draw up the specification, write the items and edit them. In both cases, it is assumed that the organisation responsible for developing the test would service the committees and provide them with expert advice on test construction. The existence of three different committees presupposes the existence of experienced item writers and editors, and runs the risk that the tests being constructed will reflect the isolation in which each group has worked. Clearly, there ought to be overall supervision, and it would seem inevitable that this should be exercised by the specification committee. The use of a single larger committee would mean that every member would have the opportunity of taking part in every aspect of test construction, an opportunity which is very important at a time when comparatively few people have the relevant experience. It would also have the effect of identifying, for the future, those with particular skill in editing or item writing. On the other hand, the work of the single committee may well be slow, and the final test may show signs of the somewhat less rigorous approach adopted.

While it is important to emphasise that no hard and fast procedures ought to be laid down, a compromise between the two extremes would seem to have a great deal to recommend it. Here, the specification committee would concern itself with drawing up the specification and with editing the items, but the actual editorial work would be carried out by a sub-committee of between, say, three and five members rather than the full committee. In this way, the full committee would be able to keep a general eye upon the whole process of the development of the test with which they were concerned. The item writing, on the other hand, would be carried out by people outside the committee, working upon the specifications laid down by the committee. A preliminary edit could be carried out by post, by which means items from all writers could be circulated for comment and the subsequent comments also circulated, with the testing organisation acting as post office. This procedure would greatly improve the quality of the items and save the time of the committee at the final stages of editing. Such a preliminary edit would be particularly valuable when inexperienced item writers were participating. The decision as to which course to adopt is obviously one for the group or body responsible for construc-ing the test.

It is not possible, of course, to provide a complete blueprint for editing, but all the items should be read carefully to see:

1   that their structure does not contain any mistakes
2   that their location on the specification grid is correct
3   that they achieve their aim, i.e. that they test something worth while and that they test the ability which they are intended to test.

In saying this it should be emphasised that there are no absolute standards of correctness. Every item can be improved.

1   In considering the structure of the item, the following points should be looked for:

a) that the answer keyed as correct *is* correct
b) that none of the distractors could be regarded as correct
c) that none of the distractors is so inappropriate in rela-tion to the stem as to attract virtually no answers
d) that the options are parallel in the sense in which this term has previously been defined
e) that the information contained in the question is accurate
f) that the question is asked as briefly and concisely as possible
g) that there is no ambiguity in the wording.

This list is by no means exhaustive but is intended to under-line the most important points.

2   As regards the place of the item on the grid, this is solely a matter of inspection linked with knowledge of the subjects and the skills being tested.

3   In considering the aim of the item disagreements can arise, since the answers to items may be arrived at differently by different people; for example, one person may know the answer as a fact and another may arrive at it by deduction. It is important here to consider the item in terms of those who are going to answer it; this emphasises the importance of the practising teacher being involved in item writing and editing. In all cases editorial comment must be constructive, and item writers, particularly when they are starting to write items, must be prepared to accept very stringent criticism without worrying too much that their favourite brainchild has been either demolished or changed beyond recognition.

The items which have survived have now to be assembled into a pre-test form based on the original specification grid. Before starting upon this task it is advisable to type all the items which are to be used in the assembly on to a set of 6 in. × 4 in. cards. The place of each item on the specification grid should be indicated by the use of the number/letter code shown on the grid. Finally, the constructor's estimate of the difficulty of the question should be stated (this may, of course, have been changed during the editing of the items). It is suggested that these be shown on the cards in pencil, since the pre-test may prove the estimate to be inaccurate. The cards can then be shuffled as required.

Test assembly is a skilled job and is obviously one which also requires practice. It is suggested that the following stages be adopted in the assembly of a pre-test.

1   Satisfy the grid, that is to say, sort the cards into a series of sequences which eventually result in the grid being completely covered; this will involve the cards being sorted four different ways to meet the chronological, content, skills and difficulty requirements. These sorts can be done using the code letters and numbers on the cards. Although arrangements will have been made for the grid to be covered three times by the item writers, it is possible, if there has been a high rate of rejection at the editorial stage,

that a part may not be covered at all. If this happens, further items will have to be written to make good the deficiencies.

2   Any surplus items should then be eliminated. This is largely a matter of subjective judgement based upon inspection of the items.

3   The sixty items or cards which remain should then be arranged in a definite order. To achieve this may involve conflict between the test expert's ideal of a test, perhaps one where the early items are the easiest and the last the most difficult, and the subject expert, in this case the historian, who would perhaps like to see a chronological order or a division by subject matter. The solution once again must be a compromise. It may be advisable to have one or two easy items as a lead into the test and then to follow a chronological order. If a wide variety of item types is being used, there is a good case for grouping the questions by item type in order to avoid confusing the candidate with different instructions. In this test, however, it has been agreed that only two item types be used, both of which require the same instructions, so that this problem will not arise.

4   Finally, the correct options should be placed at random within each item. One way of doing this, where the items contain four options, is to take a pack of cards, designate A as Spades, B as Hearts, C as Clubs and D as Diamonds, and after shuffling them thoroughly turn over the pack card by card, making the correct option the letter corresponding to the suit which is turned up. The only exception to a random placing of the options occurs when the options themselves form a logical sequence—when, for example, they are dates or numbers. In this case the earliest or smallest should be placed first and the latest or largest last.

The test is now ready to be reproduced for the pre-test. The description given above has assumed that only one form or version of the test is being assembled for the pre-test, but in practice it is almost certain that several forms will be assembled. This will not affect the procedures used, except that some items common to more than one form of the test may be included. About two months is a reasonable time for the test assembly stage, but this will need to be flexible in the light of the time available and the amount of work being undertaken at any given time. The way in which the test is to be presented to the candidate is discussed in the next chapter. At this stage, however, three points should be noted.

1 The instructions for answering the test, whether this is to be done on a separate answer sheet or within the body of the test booklet, should be both detailed and clear.
2 Adequate space should be given between each item, and no item should appear half on one page and half on another.
3 The candidate should be in no doubt as to whether or not there is a penalty to be imposed or a correction applied for guessing.

It is essential that candidates should be made completely aware of everything that they are required to do or not to do, and that the test itself be presented to them as simply and as clearly as possible.

The concept of item difficulty has been mentioned more than once, and it is treated in detail in chapter 4. There are, however, two important points about item difficulty which are relevant to item writing and which need to be discussed here. First, the difficulty of an item is its difficulty in relation to the group for which the test has been designed, that is, the class actually taught by the teacher or the sample of the population who will be taking the external test. Secondly, the difficulty of any item is not determined solely by the difficulty of the idea upon which it is based. The way in which the item has been phrased or the skill with which the distractors have been con- structed will affect item difficulty. To take a simple example: if we wish to elicit the date of the Battle of Agincourt, it is more difficult for a candidate to answer the item if the options read 1413, 1414, 1415, 1416 than it is if the options read 1400, 1415,

1430, 1445. This in turn is more difficult than if the options read 1400–24, 1425–49, 1450–74, 1475–99. Finally, this in its turn is more difficult than if the options read 13th century, 14th century, 15th century, 16th century. This can be demonstrated by trying out such a progression on a group of children, although a more difficult item could with advantage be selected.

We now come to the pre-testing of the printed and assembled test. The basic aim of the pre-test is to find out information about the test before it is used in an actual examination, that is to say, an examination where the results will count. One of the great drawbacks of a system of testing which employs only an essay form is the difficulty of pre-testing. Thus one usually analyses the results after the test has been taken and endeavours to adjust the marks after the marking has been completed, neither of which is really satisfactory. For a pre-test to provide information which is useful, it is important that it be carried out on a scientifically selected sample, which is as representative as possible of the candidates who will be sitting the test proper. In selecting the group such factors as type of school, geographical distribution, age and sex of candidates and level of ability should be taken into consideration. For an examining board setting an external examination, the sample should probably comprise at least 250 candidates and preferably 300 plus for each form of the test being used. There is no hard and fast rule about this; the important criterion is that the chosen sample should be representative for the test in question. For an examining board, selecting the sample for the pre-test will be in some ways easier and in others more difficult than it will be for the classroom teacher. It will be easier because greater numbers will be more readily available, and more difficult because there will be greater variety both in type of candidate and in their geographical distribution. Classroom teachers cannot, of course, easily find 100 pupils for a pre-test, let alone 300. They ought to aim at between thirty and fifty, ideally complete classes of approximately the same age, sex and ability range, in a similar type of school to their own. This again underlines the vital importance of co-operation, which is the bedrock upon which any successful test is constructed.

The pre-test will enable the test constructors to find out a number of things important to ensure that the final test is as fair as possible to all the candidates, both in its construction and in its timing. These are:

1 the difficulty of each item
2 the discriminating power of each item
3 the reliability of the test as a whole
4 the way in which each option in a multiple-choice item has functioned
5 the best time allocation for the test.

The question of item analysis, which involves the first four points, is discussed in the next chapter, and a simple procedure is described which can be carried out by the classroom teacher and which can, at the same time, give the professional test constructor the information he needs.

The other piece of information which the pre-test will provide concerns the timing of the test. How much time should be allowed for answering all the items in the test? It has been assumed that one hour is a suitable time for a test containing sixty items, but a decision must be taken as to the time allocation for the pre-test. Whatever time is chosen, it is important that all the candidates be asked to note the times at which they started and completed the pre-test. This will give the test constructors the relevant information. The time allocation decided upon for the final test should be one which allows at least 90 per cent of the candidates to complete the test.

When a test is being constructed for the first time, and in consequence no bank of pre-tested items exists, it is necessary to pre-test all the items which have survived the editorial stages. The method used to do this will to some extent depend on the number of these items. If there are enough to construct more than one complete form of the test, this should be done, and the two or three forms of the test should all be separately pre-tested. Initially, however, it is possible that a substantial

proportion of the items will fall by the wayside before the pre-
test stage is reached, and the test constructor may thus be left
with approximately 100 items out of the original 180 or so
which were written. Although he could produce a single test
with these 100 items, either as a sixty-item test plus forty
additional items or as a single 100-item test, this raises considerable problems and is of doubtful value. For example, if a
100-item test is constructed, the candidate will not be pre-
testing the actual test pattern which will later be used, and
different instructions will be required. In addition, the timing
will be different. If, on the other hand, there is a sixty-item test
followed by forty further items, there are the problems of how
these extra forty items are to be arranged and of how to ensure
that the candidates are properly motivated and take the same
trouble over the extra items as they take with the test itself.

In these circumstances it is far better to prepare two different forms of the test with a number of common items, as this
will enable a comparison to be made between performance on
the common items and performance on the different items.
Further information will thus be gained about item difficulty.
Even where there are sufficient items to construct several
completely different forms of the test, it is worth while in-
cluding a few common items. When different forms are used,
these should be randomly distributed among the candidates
taking the pre-test. The final test will then be assembled from
the versions of the pre-test, and the remaining items will form
the nucleus of an item bank for future tests. This bank should
be constantly added to, and additional items can be pre-tested
as extra items during an actual administration of the test or by
using the procedure suggested above.

All information from the pre-test should be recorded on
the item cards, i.e. indices of item facility and item discrimination and the responses made to each option where this is appropriate. While it is perfectly possible to photocopy the cards
for the full specification committee, who will need to meet to
consider the evidence of the pre-test, it would be much more
useful for them to have the information on the test itself. This

can be done by writing the details opposite each item and then having it reproduced.

The main task of this meeting will be to look at those items which the pre-test has revealed as being unsatisfactory, and having established the cause of failure—which on most occasions will be obvious—to decide whether to revise or reject the faulty items. In general, if the alteration is a small one, it is worth making; if not, it is probably better to replace the item. Any rejected item will need to be replaced by a pre-tested item conforming to a similar specification as far as the grid is concerned. The meeting will also need to look at the overall reliability of the test and to decide whether this is satisfactory or not. In any consideration of tests and items, it should always be borne in mind that there may be good reasons, from the subject point of view, why items which are apparently too easy or too difficult or which discriminate badly should be included. Thus items should not necessarily be re-jected on purely statistical grounds if there are good subject reasons for retaining them. A decision will also need to be taken on the time allocation for the final version of the test.

Following this meeting, which it is suggested should not take more than a day, the assembly of the final test will take place. In the case of an external examination those responsible for this work are certain to be members of the professional staff of the organising body. The procedures here are the same as those used for assembling the pre-test, except that there will now be a greater amount of information available on each item. The form in which the test is to be presented to the candidates—whether, for example, they will be marking their answers in a booklet or on a separate sheet of paper, and whether a correction is or is not to be made for guessing—has not been dealt with in this chapter, but will be covered later. Indeed, decisions on these points depend on a number of factors—such as the method of scoring—which will almost certainly be matters of policy for the body or group responsible for con-structing the test. They are, however, matters which those responsible for writing and editing the items will need to be aware of, even if they themselves are not asked to take decisions upon them. It is, of course, of vital importance to ensure that the format which it is intended to adopt in the final test should be tried out in the pre-test, although alterations can be made if the pre-test reveals anything as unsatisfactory.

CHAPTER 4

Item analysis

The function of a test is to provide a distribution of marks or scores which correctly reflects the distribution of abilities in the group being tested. In so far as the test does this, it is considered to be a good test; otherwise it is a poor test. The success with which the test achieves this function is referred to as its 'validity'. A valid test is one which successfully measures what it is designed to measure.

It is axiomatic in educational measurement that abilities are normally distributed in the population from which the sample group taking the test has been drawn. Thus, in a representative sample, most candidates will be of average ability with fewer above and below average and a minority who are either outstanding or hopeless. The distribution of abilities for the population or the representative sample conforms to the familiar normal or 'bell-shaped' curve shown in figure 1a. It follows that a valid test of ability will give an equally normal distribution of marks or scores as in figure 1b.

It is not difficult to envisage a test which is so easy that all the candidates produce correct responses, or one which is so difficult that no correct responses are obtained. The distribution of marks in these extreme cases will be single vertical lines located at the 100 per cent or 0 per cent marks respectively, as in figures 1c and 1d. Such extreme distributions do not reflect the true distribution of abilities that the test was designed to measure, nor would tests which erred towards these extremes, as in figures 1e and 1f. None of these tests would be valid as being a good objective measure of ability.

The expectation of a normal distribution is less likely if the group of candidates being tested is small—less than thirty, say—and not specially chosen to be representative of the population.

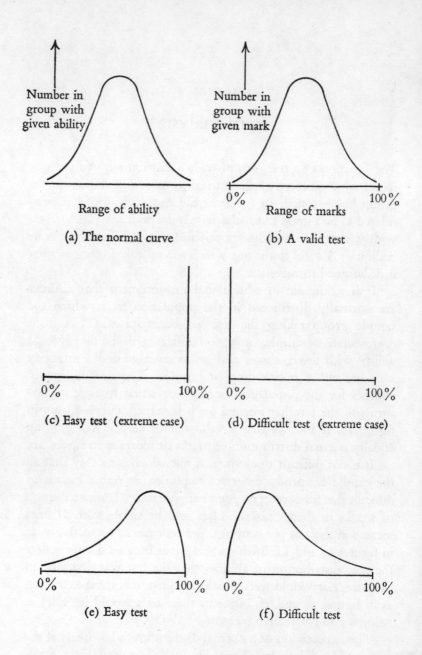

Figure 1. Marks and abilities

This is more often the rule rather than the exception with groups based on classes inside a particular school. If, however, the test taken has been validated with a much larger and representative sample of the common population, the distribution of marks is likely to be a fairly true reflection of the abilities of the group, in spite of the general lack of normality. It is important to realise, however, that test validation cannot be carried out using the marks obtained from small and unrepresentative groups of candidates.

Because individual candidates vary in their abilities, a test must reflect this in the marks awarded. This discrimination cannot be achieved unless each item in the test elicits responses which discriminate between candidates. Items must not be too easy or too difficult. If all the candidates give a correct response to an item, the item will have failed to discriminate between the candidates; and too many such items will result in the test as a whole being quite useless. A similar argument holds for too difficult items.

An item at about the right level of difficulty will be one for which approximately 50 per cent of the candidates give a correct response. For this item the candidates will be separated into two groups, the correct and the incorrect, with roughly equal numbers in each. A similar division takes place for each of the other items making up the test, although in general the division will not each time concern the same candidates in each group. Thus, when the sum total for all the items is obtained, a distribution of marks or scores is found which will roughly conform to the normal curve, most candidates obtaining average scores with few very high and few very low scores.

The correct level of difficulty of an item is not, however, the only requirement for a valid test. Discrimination is also needed; that is to say, in a valid test one would expect to find a greater proportion of correct responses from the candidates of high ability than from the candidates of low ability. The measure of the discrimination of an item is achieved by measuring the association between the candidate separation for *the item* and that for *the test as a whole*. Statistically this is done by calculating the point biserial correlation for each item; this topic is dealt with in advanced books on statistics such as Garrett's (1958) *Statistics in Psychology and Education*. It is possible, however, to measure the degree of discrimination of each item in a simpler though slightly less rigorous way; the simplified procedure will be described here.

Three statistics are required if we are to consider in a meaningful way the acceptability of items and the appropriateness of the test as a whole for the purpose for which it was designed. These are:

 a) the item difficulty
 b) the item discrimination
 c) the test reliability.

It is also important where multiple-choice items are used to know the pattern of responses obtained for each option.

The item difficulty

The difficulty of an item is usually expressed by its degree of facility or *facility index* (F). If the value of F is high, the item is an easy one; if it is low, the item is a difficult one. The facility index of an item is defined as the percentage of all candidates making a correct or appropriate response to the item. Thus, if the total number of candidates taking the test is 200, and 80 make a correct response to a particular item, the facility index of this item is 40 per cent, i.e. $F = 40\%$. If 150 make a correct response to another item, the facility index of this item will be 75 per cent, i.e. $F = 75\%$.

In parts of the literature on this subject, the facility index as defined in the previous paragraph is referred to as the difficulty index. This is somewhat confusing in that it is the percentage of *correct* responses which is measured and not the percentage of *incorrect* responses. High values of the so-called difficulty index go with absence of difficulty rather than presence of difficulty. For this reason, facility index appears to be a more satisfactory term for what is being measured.

The item discrimination

If the items making up the test have been carefully framed to test the defined objectives of the particular course of study and if they are representative of the kinds of ability to be tested, the total score obtained on the test is likely to be fairly close to the required assessment of ability it is designed to measure. High scores will generally denote high ability and low scores low ability. It is essential, however, to ensure that each individual item is discriminating between the candidates in much the same way as the discrimination resulting from the final total scores.

The final total scores permit the arrangement of the candidates in a rank order from the highest to the lowest. Equal groups are selected at the top and bottom ends of the scale, and these constitute the high and low ability groups. In practice, the top 27 per cent and the bottom 27 per cent are chosen for this purpose, or as close to this percentage as possible. If each item discriminates between candidates in a similar manner to the test as a whole, we should expect a greater number of correct responses to a given item in the top 27 per cent group than in the bottom 27 per cent group. If the number of correct responses is the same for both groups, the item has failed to discriminate between the candidates of high and the candidates of low ability, and thus it has made no contribution to the final distribution of marks or scores. Such an item could be left out without affecting the final rank order of the candidates and would be considered a poor item.

It may be asked why 27 per cent is chosen for this purpose and not 25 per cent or 20 per cent, or some more reasonable-looking percentage. Research has shown that 27 per cent provides the best compromise between making the extreme groups as large as possible and making them as different as possible. 27 per cent appears to be the optimum value, the use of which enables it to be said with confidence that the selected upper group will be superior in ability to the selected lower group. At the same time, it provides an adequate sample upon which to carry out calculations. It is not necessary, however, to be slavish in this, and the practical objective of selecting good items and rejecting poor items can be reasonably well served by an approximation to the optimum 27 per cent value.

We can define a *discrimination index* (D) for an item as follows:

$$\text{Discrimination index } (D) = \frac{(N_H - N_L)}{n}$$

where N_H is the number of correct responses in the top 27 per cent,
N_L is the number of correct responses in the bottom 27 per cent,
n is the number of candidates constituting 27 per cent of the entry, i.e. the number in each group.

The degree of facility, or facility index, has been defined as the percentage of *all* the candidates who make a correct response to the item. If attention is concentrated on the top and bottom 27 per cent groups of those taking the test, an approximation to the facility index can be found by determining the percentage of correct responses in the 54 per cent group so selected. Using the notation above, we have

$$\text{Facility index } (F) = \frac{(N_H + N_L)}{2n} \times 100\%$$

It should be noted that if all the top 27 per cent give a correct response to an item and none of the bottom 27 per cent give a correct response, the discrimination index for the item is 1·0. This is the maximum degree of discrimination possible. If the number of correct responses in each group is the same, the discrimination index is zero. Such an item fails to discriminate and is a poor item in consequence. It is possible for the discrimination index to be negative when the number of correct responses is greater for the bottom 27 per cent than it is for the top 27 per cent. This does not happen often, provided that care has been taken in the design of the item, but if it does it means that the item is at variance in its discrimination when compared with the discrimination of the test as a whole. The two main reasons for this are faulty wording of items, which leads to ambiguity, and items which encourage guessing by the candidates because they are too difficult.

There is no reason to suppose that candidates of low ability should fare worse in guessing correctly than candidates of high ability if all are forced to guess by a poorly constructed item. An item with a negative discrimination index would almost certainly be rejected.

In the case of multiple-choice items, it is useful additional information to have the degree of response to the distracting options as well as the facility and discrimination of the item as a whole. This information assists in the choice of suitable options. Consider the following example:

The 1832 Parliamentary Reform Act was important because

A it deprived the landed gentry of their influence in Parliament

B it more than doubled the electorate

C it introduced voting by secret ballot

D it laid the foundation upon which subsequent Reform Acts were based.

The correct response to this item is D. The other options are distractors. If we suppose that 200 candidates took this test, giving 54 in the top 27 per cent and 54 in the bottom 27 per cent, the responses to this item might be found to be as follows:

Responses

Option	Top 27%	Bottom 27%
A	12	26
B	3	8
C	1	6
D	38 (N_H)	14 (N_L)
Omitted	0	0

The number of correct responses is 52, 38 being in the top group and 14 in the bottom group. $N_H = 38$ and $N_L = 14$. The facility index for this item is therefore $(52/108)\ 100 = 48\%$, i.e. $F = 48\%$. The discrimination index is $(38 - 14)/54 =$

$24/54 = 0.44$, i.e. $D = 0.44$. This multiple-choice item would be considered acceptable, as we shall see later. However, the responses to the distractor options are equally informative.

It is quite clear that very few candidates thought options B or C plausible alternatives. The degree of distraction of these options was not very high. One possible reason for this is that, while options A and D are points of general significance, options B and C are definite facts which many candidates at this level would know to be incorrect. Where implausible options exist, candidates can readily eliminate them and thus narrow the margin of choice. A multiple-choice item with four or five options becomes effectively a two- or three-choice item. In this example it might be worth revising or replacing options B and C and subjecting the item to a further pre-test.

The purpose of item analysis is to enable the test constructor to distinguish between good and poor items. In this context, the criteria of 'good' and 'poor' have specific and definable meanings. A good item is one which is at roughly the correct level of difficulty and has sufficiently high discrimination. For practical purposes this is considered to be an item for which the facility index falls between 40 per cent and 60 per cent, and for which the discrimination index exceeds 0.4.

Those items with a facility index of more than 60 per cent err on the easy side, and those with a facility index of less than 40 per cent err on the too difficult side. Further, items with a discrimination index of between 0.30 and 0.39 are reasonable, but can usually be improved; between 0.20 and 0.29 are marginal and usually require substantial revision; below 0.20 the items must be rejected as being completely unsuitable. Items with a negative discrimination index would come in this last category. Those items which analysis suggests are really unsuitable are probably better abandoned altogether rather than patched up. The Americans call patched up items 're-treads', and in order to get a satisfactory retread the original tyre casing needs to be sound.

The requirements outlined in the previous paragraph may be seen more clearly in a table.

Discrimination index (D)	Facility index (F)		
	Below 40%	40%–60%	Above 60%
Above 0·40	Difficult★	Acceptable★	Easy★
0·30–0·39	Difficult	Improvable	Easy
0·20–0·29	Difficult	Marginal	Easy
Below 0·20	Rejected	Rejected	Rejected

The items which fall into the categories marked with an asterisk (★) would normally be acceptable items for the test. A few easy or difficult items may be included in the test, provided that the discrimination is reasonable. Indeed, there is something to be said for some of the early items in a test being on the easy side in order to help the candidate to relax. Similarly, a few difficult items would serve the function of stretching the more able candidates. In general, very easy and very difficult items have poor discrimination, and too many of these items would have a serious effect on the overall reliability and the validity of the test. The number of easy and difficult items introduced should therefore be kept to a minimum, though there is no hard and fast rule on what this minimum might be. The only satisfactory indication that the number introduced has become excessive is provided by the reliability coefficient for the test. The calculation of a reliability coefficient is described below.

The assessment of the acceptability of items should be related to the particular population for which the test is designed, and for no other. A good item for one population may be a poor one for another, and vice versa. To ask a population of physics graduates to indicate the correct form of Shrödinger's Wave Equation may prove acceptable. It would be quite unacceptable for a population comprising those taking O level physics. It is for this reason that the sample chosen for the pre-test needs to be fully representative of the population from which it has been drawn, and for which the test is being designed. This cannot be stressed too often.

There is sometimes confusion between a representative sample and a random sample. A random sample is chosen from a population in a random manner, usually by a method based on the system of random numbers. A random sample is free from bias and a necessary prerequisite for valid statistical analysis. Such a sample, however, may not always be representative of the population. This is expecially true of a population formed by clearly identifiable sub-groups present in different proportions. A representative sample will reflect the same proportions of the sub-groups as exist in the population. Each proportion, however, will be chosen at random from the particular sub-group. This procedure is referred to as stratified random sampling and may best be illustrated by an example.

Let us suppose that a survey is to be carried out among the spectators at a football match on the adequacy of the facilities at the ground. A random sample might give a majority of spectators from the grandstand and few from the terraces, and so would not be representative of the population of spectators. On the other hand, if it was known that 8 per cent were grandstand spectators, 40 per cent were on the covered terraces, and 52 per cent on open terraces, random samples could be taken from each group in the same proportion to provide a representative sample. Thus, if the sample consisted of 100 spectators, 8 would have been chosen at random from the stands, 40 at random from the covered terraces and 52 at random from the open terraces. A survey based on this sample is likely to be more representative of the population of spectators as a whole than one based on a purely random sample.

The test reliability

If a test has been designed and validated for a particular group of candidates, is it likely to be equally valid for another and comparable group of candidates? To what extent is the test reliable as a measure of ability? The reliability of a test may be assessed in a number of ways, and the reader is referred to advanced texts for a discussion of these. A quick method which can be used with the 27 per cent grouping employed in finding the discrimination index is one developed by Kuder and

Richardson. This provides a reliability coefficient for the test as a whole. The higher this coefficient is, the more reliable it is likely to be, and in academic achievement tests one ought to achieve a reliability coefficient, $r = 0\cdot8$ or higher.

Figure 2 shows a typical item analysis sheet which is used to facilitate the calculation of the three basic statistics: the facility index of each item, the discrimination of each item, and the reliability coefficient for the test as a whole. In the example there are assumed to be 15 items in the test and that it was taken by 28 candidates. 27 per cent of 28 is near enough 7. The top 7 candidates on the test as a whole are designated A to G, and the bottom 7 T to Z. Against each candidate the correct responses given to the items are represented by ticks.

These numbers have been deliberately kept small for the purposes of illustration, and it is appreciated that in practice they are likely to be very much larger.

PROCEDURE

1 For each item add up the number of correct responses in the top group, inserting the totals in the row labelled N_H.

2 Repeat for the bottom group, inserting totals in row labelled N_L.

3 Calculate the total percentage of correct responses for each item and insert in row labelled $F(\%)$. *This gives the facility index for each item.* An approximation to F can be found by using the percentage for the 54 per cent sample on the sheet, i.e.

$$\frac{(N_H + N_L)}{2n} \times 100$$

where n is the number of candidates in the 27 per cent group.

4 Insert the values of $(N_H - N_L)$ for each item in the row so labelled.

5 Evaluate $\dfrac{(N_H - N_L)}{n}$ for each item and insert in row labelled D. *This row gives the value of the discrimination index for each item.*

Candidate \ Item	1	2	3	4	5	6	7	8	9	10	11	12	13	14	15
A	✓	✓	✓	✓		✓	✓	✓	✓	✓	✓	✓	✓	✓	✓
B	✓		✓		✓	✓	✓	✓	✓	✓	✓	✓	✓	✓	✓
C	✓	✓	✓		✓		✓	✓		✓	✓	✓	✓	✓	✓
D	✓	✓	✓	✓	✓		✓	✓	✓	✓	✓	✓	✓		
E		✓	✓		✓	✓		✓		✓	✓	✓		✓	✓
F	✓	✓		✓	✓		✓	✓	✓	✓			✓	✓	
G	✓	✓	✓			✓	✓	✓	✓	✓			✓		
N_H	6	6	6	3	5	4	6	7	5	7	5	5	6	5	4
T		✓	✓	✓	✓			✓		✓					
U	✓			✓	✓	✓			✓	✓					
V			✓		✓		✓		✓					✓	✓
W		✓		✓		✓		✓	✓				✓		
X	✓		✓		✓	✓					✓				
Y		✓		✓			✓		✓						✓
Z			✓		✓	✓								✓	✓
N_L	2	3	4	4	5	4	2	2	4	2	1	0	1	2	3
$(N_H - N_L)$	4	3	2	−1	0	0	4	5	1	5	4	5	5	3	1
$F(\%)$*	57	64	71	50	71	57	57	64	64	64	43	36	50	50	50
D	0·57	0·43	0·29	−0·14	0	0	0·57	0·71	0·14	0·71	0·57	0·71	0·71	0·43	0·14

	1	2	3	4	5	6	7	8	9	10	11	12	13	14	15	
$(N_H - N_L)$	4	3	2	−1	0	0	4	5	1	5	4	5	5	3	1	$\dfrac{\Sigma(N_H - N_L)}{41}$
$(N_H + N_L)$	8	9	10	7	10	8	8	9	9	9	6	5	7	7	7	$\dfrac{\Sigma(N_H + N_L)}{119}$
$(N_H + N_L)^2$	64	81	100	49	100	64	64	81	81	81	36	25	49	49	49	$\dfrac{\Sigma(N_H + N_L)^2}{973}$

Number of items, $k = 15$ Number in 27 per cent group, $n = 7$

Reliability coefficient $= 0·41$

* Facility index values based on approximate estimate for 54 per cent sample.

Figure 2. Item analysis sheet

6 Evaluate $(N_H - N_L)$, $(N_H + N_L)$ and $(N_H + N_L)^2$ for each item, and insert in the appropriate rows at foot of table.

7 Sum up the values for each of these rows. The sum of all the $(N_H - N_L)$ values is denoted by $\sum (N_H - N_L)$ and similarly for the others.

8 Substitute values in the Kuder-Richardson formula for the reliability coefficient, r:

$$r = \frac{k}{(k-1)}\left\{1 - \frac{2n\sum(N_H + N_L) - \sum (N_H + N_L)^2}{0 \cdot 667[\sum (N_H - N_L)]^2}\right\}$$

where k is the number of items in the test and the other quantities have already been defined above.

When the procedure for item analysis has been carried out, it is possible to extract from the item analysis sheet the relevant statistics and to list these as an item summary. This summary lists all the items together with their facility and discrimination indices and records the test reliability coefficient. In this way the test may be evaluated.

Item summary sheet

Item	F(%)	D	Evaluation
1	57	0·57	Acceptable
2	64	0·43	A little too easy
3	71	0·29	Easy: poor discrimination
4	50	—0·14	Reject
5	71	0	Reject
6	57	0	Reject
7	57	0·57	Acceptable
8	64	0·71	A little too easy
9	64	0·14	Reject
10	64	0·71	A little too easy
11	43	0·57	Acceptable
12	36	0·71	A little too difficult
13	50	0·71	Acceptable
14	50	0·43	Acceptable
15	50	0·14	Reject

Reliability coefficient = 0·41 Poor

Inspection of the summary sheet shows that items 1, 7, 11, 13 and 14 are acceptable items in that they have the acceptable degree of difficulty and discrimination. Similarly, items 4, 5, 6, 9 and 15 need to be rejected as being poor in discrimination power, so poor, in fact, that adequate revision of these items seems unlikely. The remaining items could be improved by suitable revision. A close scrutiny of these items may well reveal where weaknesses have occurred. In some cases the only revision needed may be in the wording of the item.

The reliability of the test as a whole is poor, which is not surprising as it includes more than an acceptable number of very poor items. The reliability coefficient can be improved by replacing the poor items with better ones and revising those which are marginal. In this context it is important to mention that the Kuder-Richardson formula for calculating the reliability coefficient is only valid for tests which give ample time for the candidates to make their responses. It cannot be used for speed tests. The kind of objective tests envisaged for the assessment of academic attainment, however, should never be speed tests; adequate time should be given to deal with all the items.

It is important when building up a collection of acceptable items to include with the facility and discrimination indices a note of the type of group tested (e.g. 13–14 years, VI form, etc.) and also the particular ability being tested by the item (e.g. knowledge, application, etc.). The item analysis statistics are quite meaningless unless the characteristics of the candidates taking the test or pre-test are known.

The item analysis described will provide the test constructor with all the basic information he needs. It will tell him the difficulty of each item and its discriminatory power, and it will give him enough information to see whether individual options are doing their proper work. In constructing an external test which is widely taken and where the results will have important consequences for the candidates, it may be felt necessary to obtain further information by a more elaborate item analysis, particularly upon the way in which the options have performed. Such a method is illustrated in *Multiple-Choice Questions: A Close Look*, in which the candidates are divided into fifths according to their performance on the test as a whole and the responses to each item for each fifth are set out in a chart. A similar method where the candidates are divided into sixths is described in *The Certificate of Secondary Education: An Introduction to Some Techniques of Examining* (Secondary School Examinations Council 1964). In this way, faulty items, and faulty options which fail to discriminate adequately, can be identified at a glance. The nature of the item analysis carried out is entirely a matter for those constructing the test to decide upon, but the method described in this chapter is more than adequate for the majority of tests.

CHAPTER 5

Taking the test

Not very much has yet been said about that all-important individual, the candidate. In 'Taking the test', however, John and Jane Smith become the central figures. For the candidates there are, as we have mentioned, three main differences between objective tests and essay tests; these are worth repeating, since this chapter is largely concerned with how they affect the candidates in practice. First, the candidates will be required to write a great deal less—indeed, hardly at all—since the items require them to read and think rather than think and write. Secondly, the test will be presented to them in quite a different form from that to which they are accustomed. It will come in a booklet which may or may not contain an answer sheet, and they will be required to mark this booklet or answer sheet in accordance with a given set of instructions. Thirdly, they will be asked to answer many more questions than they answer in the external tests with which they are familiar.

The candidates' whole approach to the test must, therefore, be different, and their thinking on matters such as the time they can afford to allow for each question will need to be reconsidered. As the format of the objective tests becomes more familiar, these differences will become less significant, but it is very necessary that they should be appreciated by the candidate. Here the role played both by the teacher and by those responsible for the construction of the test is all-important. Two points need emphasising here. First, the candidate must be given, not only at the time the test is taken, but beforehand, clear and concise instructions which cover everything he needs to know. Different methods can be used to achieve this, but there is a good case for producing a booklet for each candidate. This could describe very briefly the construction of the test, the form that the test will take and the way in which the candidates will be required to answer the questions. Such a booklet should give them advice on how to allocate their time, and should conclude with a series of sample questions and an answer sheet in order that they can practise them realistically. It is worth considering, too, the production of a booklet for the teacher, which covers some of the points mentioned in the candidates' booklet. The amount of preliminary information provided will almost certainly diminish as objective tests become more widely used, but it is to be hoped that those concerned with setting such tests will not neglect to keep teachers and candidates fully informed.

The second point is that it should be made clear to the teacher as well as to the candidate that practising objective test questions is only useful as a means of becoming familiar with the format and not with the actual questions. The kind of question spotting with its emphasis upon model answers, which is so often used in preparation for tests consisting of essays, will achieve very little indeed in an objective test. The number of questions in an objective test ensures a wide content coverage, and thus makes question spotting both difficult and useless. The best kind of preparation for an objective test is to know the subject—as it is, indeed, for any type of test.

If, therefore, candidates have been provided with the kind of information mentioned above, they will enter the examination hall to sit the test familiar with its format, and with some knowledge of the thinking behind it and the work that has gone into its preparation. On taking their places they will find not the usual separate question paper and answer booklet, but a sealed booklet of about quarto size, which will contain the questions together with instructions for answering them, either in the booklet itself or on a separate answer sheet enclosed. They will also each be given an india rubber and a soft lead pencil. At the top right-hand corner of the booklet there will be a serial number, since every copy of a secure objective test is numbered for the purposes of identification. This number will also be repeated on the answer sheet, if there is one.

On the outside of the booklet there will be the title of the test, the time to be taken, and the name of the organisation responsible for constructing the test. The general instructions for the test will probably be printed on the outside of the front page, although testing organisations, of course, vary on matters of detail.

The instructions should include:

1   the time allocated for the test, or for each section if the test is divided into sections
2   the number of questions which the test contains
3   information on whether a correction for guessing is to be applied or not
4   details of the information required from the candidate, for example, name, sex and school
5   instructions for marking the test booklet or answer sheet together with examples of every type of question which is to be used in the test
6   instructions for erasing incorrect answers.

(A set of such instructions is shown later in the chapter.)

These six points contain a number of important matters which should be considered in greater detail; they will be mentioned in turn. For this purpose, the history test, which has been our example so far, will continue to be used.

The first two points—the time and the number of questions—are completely straightforward, and the instructions would read: 'This is a 60-minute test containing 60 questions'. It will be noted that the word 'question' and not 'item' has been used throughout this chapter and in the instructions. This is deliberate. To those constructing the test it is an item to which the candidate selects a response, but to the candidate it is a question which he answers either correctly or incorrectly.

The third point raises the whole question of guessing in objective testing, and the instructions given will vary according to the decision taken on this matter by those responsible for constructing the test. Before the decision is taken, the whole problem of guessing needs to be discussed, since the issue is important in relation to objective tests. Critics of objective testing maintain, quite reasonably, that when candidates are presented with a number of alternative answers and are asked to select one of them as the correct answer, there is considerable encouragement to guess, and therefore unjustifiable benefit may accrue to the less good candidates. In the next few paragraphs, guessing is considered from a largely non-mathematical standpoint in relation to four questions.

1 Can one detect beyond any reasonable doubt whether a candidate has guessed in an objective test or not?
2 Does a correction formula have any effect upon the rank order of candidates?
3 Can a rubric prohibiting guessing be enforced?
4 Is guessing undesirable in itself?

1 It is practically impossible to tell if a candidate has guessed the answer to a question or not. It is perhaps possible to envisage a situation, as in a mathematics test embodying both an objective and a more traditional section, in which questions are asked in both sections testing two applications of the same formula. In the traditional section it is clear that the candidate does not understand how to apply the formula, yet in the objective section he answers the question correctly. It could be argued not unreasonably that the candidate had guessed the answer to the objective question, but can we be so sure of this that we penalise candidates arbitrarily by deducting from one and not from another? There would appear to be no justification at all for doing so. It follows, therefore, that if a correction is to be applied for guessing, it must be applied equally to all the candidates: in a test such a correction can only be applied to the evidence that the candidates present, namely, the number of their right answers or the number of their wrong answers. One either penalises the guesser or rewards the non-guesser, the former being the most commonly used method. Whatever formula is used, the scores, although different, will be perfectly correlated, providing all the candidates attempt all the questions.

2   This leads to the second point. Fairly extensive research in the United States, where the increasing tendency today is not to apply a guessing correction, suggests that scores which are corrected for guessing will nearly always rank students in about the same relative position as do the uncorrected scores. This has been confirmed by one of the authors (RBM) for objective-type tests on educational measurement taken by students of education at the University of Reading. Thus, in a test designed merely to rank the candidates there is very little practical gain for the extra work involved. In a pass/fail situation the problem is, of course, complicated, since the decision as to the pass mark will be different according to which procedure is adopted. It is worth emphasising that correction for guessing will not ensure that the lucky guesser fares as badly as the unlucky guesser or, in other words, such a correction does not ensure that the element of chance is eliminated. R. L. Ebel (1965) in his excellent book *Measuring Educational Achievement* illustrates this by the following example: thirty-two students attempt all ten items in a true/false test. Each student knows the answer to five of the ten questions. On the rest they guess, and some are inevitably luckier than others. Probability would suggest that one of the thirty-two will answer all five of the remaining questions correctly by guessing and thus obtain 10 out of 10, and that five of the thirty-two will guess four correctly and obtain 9 out of 10. At the other end of the scale a similar situation is likely to occur, namely, that five will guess the answer to one question correctly and so obtain 6 out of 10, and one will guess none correctly and his score will remain at 5. The correction formula $S = R - W$ is applied,* with the result that the differences, far from being eliminated or even reduced, are actually magnified. After correction, the candidate with a score of 10 continues to have 10, the candidate with a score of 5 is reduced to 0; those with 9 are reduced to 8, while those with 6 end up with 2. The lucky are thus further rewarded and the unlucky are penalised even more.

* S = corrected score, R = number of correct responses, W = number of incorrect responses.

Another interesting experiment quoted by Ebel, which was carried out in 1944 at Iowa by Professors Blommers and Lindquist, is also relevant here. A group of tests was administered to candidates with instructions not to guess. At the completion of the named time-limit, the candidates were asked to go through the tests again and mark with a different-coloured pencil the answers to the items they had omitted. Both sets of responses were then scored, both with and without a correction for guessing. This procedure revealed that the highest reliability was obtained when students were warned not to guess, but when no correction was applied. Clearly, this kind of deception could not be undertaken in a test in which the result was to count.

Between the two practical alternatives—namely (a) instructions not to guess and the application of a correction for guessing, and (b) instructions to answer every question and no correction for guessing—there was a slight difference in reliability in favour of the first alternative, but there was no noticeable difference in validity. The detailed tables also showed that whichever method was used there was little difference in the rank order of candidates taking the test. On this evidence, the answer to the second of the four questions asked earlier is rather inconclusive. A correction does seem to have an effect but only a very slight one, on the rank order; and it may, in addition, exaggerate the differences between candidates obtained by uncorrected scores.

3   The third question is probably the least important of the three, although it it not without relevance. In any test, but particularly in any widely taken external test, the rubric (i.e. the instructions on taking the test which the candidates are required to obey) must be enforceable by the testing organisation on all the candidates if it is to have any meaning or achieve anything useful. It is doubtful whether it is possible to enforce an instruction to candidates to answer only the questions they think they know and not to guess those they do not know, not because some candidates may deliberately disobey it and can-

not be detected—although, of course, this is a possibility—but because the candidates may interpret in different ways what constitutes guessing. Consideration of this leads inevitably to the fourth question, which is crucial.

4 Is guessing undesirable in itself? This cannot really be answered unless the word 'guessing' is defined. If by guessing we mean blind guessing, perhaps it is undesirable; but how frequently are questions answered or decisions made from blind guessing? The answer is probably very seldom; most are the result of partial knowledge. Why, therefore, should a candidate who can eliminate, say, two alternatives in a four-response multiple-choice item as a result of partial knowledge not give himself a better chance of gaining some reward for this compared with a candidate who does not know any of the four responses? Most decisions are made as a result of considering evidence which may be fragmentary and by making the most realistic appraisal of that evidence. This involves the same kind of assessment as will be employed by a candidate with partial knowledge when he is taking a test. Our existing external tests, moreover, encourage the same process, and candidates do not get penalised. Furthermore, in an objective test where candidates are required to answer some sixty questions in a period of one hour, ignorance of the answer carries its own penalty, whether the candidate tries to improve his score by guessing or not. It takes candidates longer or at least as long to discover they do not know the answer than it does to discover they do. If they then try to work it out on the basis of partial knowledge, it will take them longer than if they make an immediate blind guess, but they are more likely to achieve a better total score. This may not be a very scientific description, but it does seem to be reasonable that the candidate's final score should be achieved by his knowledge considered as a whole, even if his knowledge in a specific area may only be partial. The best way to achieve this would seem to be to encourage the candidate to attempt all the questions, and not to apply a correction for guessing. This could be done by

issuing an instruction such as the following: 'Attempt all the questions, but do not spend too much time on any one question. Remember that all the questions carry equal marks, and that your total score on the test is the number of correct answers you give.'

The fourth point requires no further explanation, though the amount of information required from candidates may possibly vary from test to test.

5 The detail provided in the instructions upon the fifth point, the recording of the answers by the candidates, will depend largely upon whether the answers are to be recorded on the test booklet or on a separate answer sheet. This decision will almost certainly be taken in the light of the method which is to be used to score the test. On all counts, it is very much more satisfactory to have the answers marked in the booklet itself. It is simpler for the candidate if the supervisor has only one set of papers to collect, thus easing the security problem, and, finally, errors are less likely to occur in the scoring. At present, however, booklets are more suitable for hand scoring than machine scoring, but since most large tests are likely to be designed eventually for machine scoring, the candidate is more likely to be asked to fill in an answer sheet rather than to answer in a booklet.

The scoring of the test is something which will be discussed in more detail in the next chapter, but it seems likely that by the early 1970s many of the present problems associated with machine scoring will be overcome, and it will be possible for all objective test answers to be recorded in the test booklet. Here, however, the detail will be based on the assumption that a separate answer sheet is used. Within each booklet to be scored in this way there will be an answer sheet stamped with the same serial number as that which appears on the booklet. An example of a commonly used type of answer sheet is shown in figure 3. The top part of the sheet contains a space upon which the candidates write their names and numbers and any other information which may be required. There may also be,

TITLE OF EXAMINING BOARD

Subject.................... Level................ Date................

Test Form No. ....

Centre Number .... ☐

Candidate's Number .... Boy

Candidate's Surname .... ☐

Candidate's Christian Names .... Girl

Do NOT write in these boxes				
1	2	3	4	5
6	7	8	9	10
11	12	13	14	15
16	17	18	19	20

1 Ⓐ Ⓑ Ⓒ Ⓓ Ⓔ	21 Ⓐ Ⓑ Ⓒ Ⓓ Ⓔ	41 Ⓐ Ⓑ Ⓒ Ⓓ Ⓔ	61 Ⓐ Ⓑ Ⓒ Ⓓ Ⓔ	81 Ⓐ Ⓑ Ⓒ Ⓓ Ⓔ
2 Ⓐ Ⓑ Ⓒ Ⓓ Ⓔ	22 Ⓐ Ⓑ Ⓒ Ⓓ Ⓔ	42 Ⓐ Ⓑ Ⓒ Ⓓ Ⓔ	62 Ⓐ Ⓑ Ⓒ Ⓓ Ⓔ	82 Ⓐ Ⓑ Ⓒ Ⓓ Ⓔ
3 Ⓐ Ⓑ Ⓒ Ⓓ Ⓔ	23 Ⓐ Ⓑ Ⓒ Ⓓ Ⓔ	43 Ⓐ Ⓑ Ⓒ Ⓓ Ⓔ	63 Ⓐ Ⓑ Ⓒ Ⓓ Ⓔ	83 Ⓐ Ⓑ Ⓒ Ⓓ Ⓔ
4 Ⓐ Ⓑ Ⓒ Ⓓ Ⓔ	24 Ⓐ Ⓑ Ⓒ Ⓓ Ⓔ	44 Ⓐ Ⓑ Ⓒ Ⓓ Ⓔ	64 Ⓐ Ⓑ Ⓒ Ⓓ Ⓔ	84 Ⓐ Ⓑ Ⓒ Ⓓ Ⓔ
5 Ⓐ Ⓑ Ⓒ Ⓓ Ⓔ	25 Ⓐ Ⓑ Ⓒ Ⓓ Ⓔ	45 Ⓐ Ⓑ Ⓒ Ⓓ Ⓔ	65 Ⓐ Ⓑ Ⓒ Ⓓ Ⓔ	85 Ⓐ Ⓑ Ⓒ Ⓓ Ⓔ
6 Ⓐ Ⓑ Ⓒ Ⓓ Ⓔ	26 Ⓐ Ⓑ Ⓒ Ⓓ Ⓔ	46 Ⓐ Ⓑ Ⓒ Ⓓ Ⓔ	66 Ⓐ Ⓑ Ⓒ Ⓓ Ⓔ	86 Ⓐ Ⓑ Ⓒ Ⓓ Ⓔ
7 Ⓐ Ⓑ Ⓒ Ⓓ Ⓔ	27 Ⓐ Ⓑ Ⓒ Ⓓ Ⓔ	47 Ⓐ Ⓑ Ⓒ Ⓓ Ⓔ	67 Ⓐ Ⓑ Ⓒ Ⓓ Ⓔ	87 Ⓐ Ⓑ Ⓒ Ⓓ Ⓔ
8 Ⓐ Ⓑ Ⓒ Ⓓ Ⓔ	28 Ⓐ Ⓑ Ⓒ Ⓓ Ⓔ	48 Ⓐ Ⓑ Ⓒ Ⓓ Ⓔ	68 Ⓐ Ⓑ Ⓒ Ⓓ Ⓔ	88 Ⓐ Ⓑ Ⓒ Ⓓ Ⓔ
9 Ⓐ Ⓑ Ⓒ Ⓓ Ⓔ	29 Ⓐ Ⓑ Ⓒ Ⓓ Ⓔ	49 Ⓐ Ⓑ Ⓒ Ⓓ Ⓔ	69 Ⓐ Ⓑ Ⓒ Ⓓ Ⓔ	89 Ⓐ Ⓑ Ⓒ Ⓓ Ⓔ
10 Ⓐ Ⓑ Ⓒ Ⓓ Ⓔ	30 Ⓐ Ⓑ Ⓒ Ⓓ Ⓔ	50 Ⓐ Ⓑ Ⓒ Ⓓ Ⓔ	70 Ⓐ Ⓑ Ⓒ Ⓓ Ⓔ	90 Ⓐ Ⓑ Ⓒ Ⓓ Ⓔ
11 Ⓐ Ⓑ Ⓒ Ⓓ Ⓔ	31 Ⓐ Ⓑ Ⓒ Ⓓ Ⓔ	51 Ⓐ Ⓑ Ⓒ Ⓓ Ⓔ	71 Ⓐ Ⓑ Ⓒ Ⓓ Ⓔ	91 Ⓐ Ⓑ Ⓒ Ⓓ Ⓔ
12 Ⓐ Ⓑ Ⓒ Ⓓ Ⓔ	32 Ⓐ Ⓑ Ⓒ Ⓓ Ⓔ	52 Ⓐ Ⓑ Ⓒ Ⓓ Ⓔ	72 Ⓐ Ⓑ Ⓒ Ⓓ Ⓔ	92 Ⓐ Ⓑ Ⓒ Ⓓ Ⓔ
13 Ⓐ Ⓑ Ⓒ Ⓓ Ⓔ	33 Ⓐ Ⓑ Ⓒ Ⓓ Ⓔ	53 Ⓐ Ⓑ Ⓒ Ⓓ Ⓔ	73 Ⓐ Ⓑ Ⓒ Ⓓ Ⓔ	93 Ⓐ Ⓑ Ⓒ Ⓓ Ⓔ
14 Ⓐ Ⓑ Ⓒ Ⓓ Ⓔ	34 Ⓐ Ⓑ Ⓒ Ⓓ Ⓔ	54 Ⓐ Ⓑ Ⓒ Ⓓ Ⓔ	74 Ⓐ Ⓑ Ⓒ Ⓓ Ⓔ	94 Ⓐ Ⓑ Ⓒ Ⓓ Ⓔ
15 Ⓐ Ⓑ Ⓒ Ⓓ Ⓔ	35 Ⓐ Ⓑ Ⓒ Ⓓ Ⓔ	55 Ⓐ Ⓑ Ⓒ Ⓓ Ⓔ	75 Ⓐ Ⓑ Ⓒ Ⓓ Ⓔ	95 Ⓐ Ⓑ Ⓒ Ⓓ Ⓔ
16 Ⓐ Ⓑ Ⓒ Ⓓ Ⓔ	36 Ⓐ Ⓑ Ⓒ Ⓓ Ⓔ	56 Ⓐ Ⓑ Ⓒ Ⓓ Ⓔ	76 Ⓐ Ⓑ Ⓒ Ⓓ Ⓔ	96 Ⓐ Ⓑ Ⓒ Ⓓ Ⓔ
17 Ⓐ Ⓑ Ⓒ Ⓓ Ⓔ	37 Ⓐ Ⓑ Ⓒ Ⓓ Ⓔ	57 Ⓐ Ⓑ Ⓒ Ⓓ Ⓔ	77 Ⓐ Ⓑ Ⓒ Ⓓ Ⓔ	97 Ⓐ Ⓑ Ⓒ Ⓓ Ⓔ
18 Ⓐ Ⓑ Ⓒ Ⓓ Ⓔ	38 Ⓐ Ⓑ Ⓒ Ⓓ Ⓔ	58 Ⓐ Ⓑ Ⓒ Ⓓ Ⓔ	78 Ⓐ Ⓑ Ⓒ Ⓓ Ⓔ	98 Ⓐ Ⓑ Ⓒ Ⓓ Ⓔ
19 Ⓐ Ⓑ Ⓒ Ⓓ Ⓔ	39 Ⓐ Ⓑ Ⓒ Ⓓ Ⓔ	59 Ⓐ Ⓑ Ⓒ Ⓓ Ⓔ	79 Ⓐ Ⓑ Ⓒ Ⓓ Ⓔ	99 Ⓐ Ⓑ Ⓒ Ⓓ Ⓔ
20 Ⓐ Ⓑ Ⓒ Ⓓ Ⓔ	40 Ⓐ Ⓑ Ⓒ Ⓓ Ⓔ	60 Ⓐ Ⓑ Ⓒ Ⓓ Ⓔ	80 Ⓐ Ⓑ Ⓒ Ⓓ Ⓔ	100 Ⓐ Ⓑ Ⓒ Ⓓ Ⓔ

Time at which test was started ....am/pm

Time at which test was finished ....am/pm

Figure 3

as there is here, a section for the use of the testing organisation, which candidates are asked not to mark in any way. The bulk of the sheet consists of the question numbers or sequence, opposite which are five circles containing the letters A B C D E. A multi-purpose sheet such as this (that is, one which the testing organisation can use for a number of different tests, particularly at the pre-test stage) is likely to contain more questions, each with more options, than may be required for a specific occasion. This is true of the answer sheet that would be required for our history test, since the multi-purpose sheet contains more than sixty questions and makes provision for five options, whereas the history test has only sixty questions and four options per question. Wherever possible, however, even at the pre-test stage, the answer sheet should be designed with a particular test in mind. This point reinforces the advantages of scoring in the test booklet itself, since differently designed answer sheets are not then needed. Nevertheless, if a multi-purpose answer sheet is used for pre-testing our history test, it must be made quite clear to the candidates that they do not use option E and that they only use questions 1 to 60. For comparison, the sheet which might be used for the history test is shown as figure 4. This has the additional advantage that the title of the test can be printed, whereas on the other sheet the candidates would be asked to fill it in themselves. For both sheets, however, the method of recording the answer is the same. When the candidates have decided on the correct answer, they fill in, with the pencil provided, the circle containing the letter which corresponds to what they think is the correct answer, making sure that they use the correct line in relation to the question number. They then move on to the next, and so on. Occasionally, the space to be filled in is a square or an oblong box, but the principle remains the same, and the scoring process, if it is mechanical, picks up the graphite mark made by the pencil.

The above description leads naturally to the sixth point of the general instructions: what to do if a mistake is made in recording the answer, or the candidate subsequently changes

NAME AND LEVEL OF SUBJECT

Date

Centre Number ....

Candidate's Number .... Boy

Candidate's Surname ....

Candidate's Christian Names .... Girl

Do NOT write in these boxes				
1	2	3	4	5
6	7	8	9	10
11	12	13	14	15
16	17	18	19	20

1 Ⓐ Ⓑ Ⓒ Ⓓ	21 Ⓐ Ⓑ Ⓒ Ⓓ	41 Ⓐ Ⓑ Ⓒ Ⓓ
2 Ⓐ Ⓑ Ⓒ Ⓓ	22 Ⓐ Ⓑ Ⓒ Ⓓ	42 Ⓐ Ⓑ Ⓒ Ⓓ
3 Ⓐ Ⓑ Ⓒ Ⓓ	23 Ⓐ Ⓑ Ⓒ Ⓓ	43 Ⓐ Ⓑ Ⓒ Ⓓ
4 Ⓐ Ⓑ Ⓒ Ⓓ	24 Ⓐ Ⓑ Ⓒ Ⓓ	44 Ⓐ Ⓑ Ⓒ Ⓓ
5 Ⓐ Ⓑ Ⓒ Ⓓ	25 Ⓐ Ⓑ Ⓒ Ⓓ	45 Ⓐ Ⓑ Ⓒ Ⓓ
6 Ⓐ Ⓑ Ⓒ Ⓓ	26 Ⓐ Ⓑ Ⓒ Ⓓ	46 Ⓐ Ⓑ Ⓒ Ⓓ
7 Ⓐ Ⓑ Ⓒ Ⓓ	27 Ⓐ Ⓑ Ⓒ Ⓓ	47 Ⓐ Ⓑ Ⓒ Ⓓ
8 Ⓐ Ⓑ Ⓒ Ⓓ	28 Ⓐ Ⓑ Ⓒ Ⓓ	48 Ⓐ Ⓑ Ⓒ Ⓓ
9 Ⓐ Ⓑ Ⓒ Ⓓ	29 Ⓐ Ⓑ Ⓒ Ⓓ	49 Ⓐ Ⓑ Ⓒ Ⓓ
10 Ⓐ Ⓑ Ⓒ Ⓓ	30 Ⓐ Ⓑ Ⓒ Ⓓ	50 Ⓐ Ⓑ Ⓒ Ⓓ
11 Ⓐ Ⓑ Ⓒ Ⓓ	31 Ⓐ Ⓑ Ⓒ Ⓓ	51 Ⓐ Ⓑ Ⓒ Ⓓ
12 Ⓐ Ⓑ Ⓒ Ⓓ	32 Ⓐ Ⓑ Ⓒ Ⓓ	52 Ⓐ Ⓑ Ⓒ Ⓓ
13 Ⓐ Ⓑ Ⓒ Ⓓ	33 Ⓐ Ⓑ Ⓒ Ⓓ	53 Ⓐ Ⓑ Ⓒ Ⓓ
14 Ⓐ Ⓑ Ⓒ Ⓓ	34 Ⓐ Ⓑ Ⓒ Ⓓ	54 Ⓐ Ⓑ Ⓒ Ⓓ
15 Ⓐ Ⓑ Ⓒ Ⓓ	35 Ⓐ Ⓑ Ⓒ Ⓓ	55 Ⓐ Ⓑ Ⓒ Ⓓ
16 Ⓐ Ⓑ Ⓒ Ⓓ	36 Ⓐ Ⓑ Ⓒ Ⓓ	56 Ⓐ Ⓑ Ⓒ Ⓓ
17 Ⓐ Ⓑ Ⓒ Ⓓ	37 Ⓐ Ⓑ Ⓒ Ⓓ	57 Ⓐ Ⓑ Ⓒ Ⓓ
18 Ⓐ Ⓑ Ⓒ Ⓓ	38 Ⓐ Ⓑ Ⓒ Ⓓ	58 Ⓐ Ⓑ Ⓒ Ⓓ
19 Ⓐ Ⓑ Ⓒ Ⓓ	39 Ⓐ Ⓑ Ⓒ Ⓓ	59 Ⓐ Ⓑ Ⓒ Ⓓ
20 Ⓐ Ⓑ Ⓒ Ⓓ	40 Ⓐ Ⓑ Ⓒ Ⓓ	60 Ⓐ Ⓑ Ⓒ Ⓓ

Time at which test was started ....am/pm

Time at which test was finished ....am/pm

Figure 4

his mind. If this happens, the first mark must be completely erased with the rubber provided, and the new choice filled in. Under no circumstances should more than one circle or space be marked. This rule always applies; even if candidates think that more than one answer is correct, they must decide upon one answer only. Filling in more than one space will automatically result in a candidate gaining no credit for that question. It is important to emphasise that the original mark must be erased with the rubber and not crossed out or crossed through with the pencil. Machine scoring works on the basis of pencil marks. The machine does not see the erasures, as a human marker would. The wording of the instructions described will vary from test to test and from organisation to organisation and, although obvious, it is important to emphasise that candidates must read and take note of the instructions for the test they are actually taking. This last sentence underlines the importance of the point made earlier, that all the questions in the test should be constructed in the same format wherever possible, otherwise it will mean not only that different instructions will have to be issued for each type used, but also that a different layout may be required for part of the answer sheet. Once again, scoring the test booklet itself has the advantage here. In the history test, it was agreed that two item forms would be used: multiple-choice and multiple-completion. These both require the same instructions, although an illustration of both types should be provided for the candidates in the test booklet. As an illustration, a set of sample instructions follows.

Sample general instructions for candidates taking an objective test

YOU HAVE FIVE MINUTES TO READ THESE INSTRUCTIONS IF YOU ARE NOT SURE OF ANY POINTS ASK THE SUPERVISOR

1 This is a 60-minute test. You should attempt all the questions, but remember that you have 60 questions to answer, so do not spend too much time on any one question. Your

score is the number of correct answers you give to the questions asked.

2   On being told to start the test, open the test booklet by breaking the seal and take out the answer sheet. Fill in your centre number, your candidate's number, your names and sex in the spaces provided. Having done this, fill in the starting time and start to answer the questions.

3   All your answers to the questions should be marked on the answer sheet and not on the test booklet itself. Against each question number on the answer sheet you will see four circles containing the letters A, B, C and D. These refer to the four possible answers provided for each question in the test booklet. After you have read the question and decided on the correct answer, fill in, with the pencil provided, the circle corresponding to your selected answer on the answer sheet.

If you change your mind or wish to amend your answer, you must completely erase your first mark with the rubber provided before filling in another circle. If you leave more than one circle filled in for any one question, you will receive no credit for that question.

Question 1 Ⓐ Ⓑ Ⓒ Ⓓ   This is correctly marked.

Question 2 Ⓐ Ⓑ Ⓒ Ⓓ   This is incorrectly marked and will not be counted.

As a further help to you, four questions of the type which will appear in the test are given as examples on the back page of this booklet. They have all been correctly answered, and it is suggested that you study these before starting the test.

4   When you have finished the test, fill in the time at which you completed the last item in the space provided at the foot of the answer sheet. If you do not finish the test, do not fill in this space.

The supervisor should, before starting the test, make a special point of drawing these instructions to the attention of all candidates and should allow them a short interval to read them. This again underlines the need for the provision of preliminary information, as there is nothing more disturbing for candidates who understand the instructions to be held up by having to listen to the questions raised by those who do not understand them. There is, indeed, something to be said for requiring the supervisor to read the instructions aloud, at least while objective tests are comparatively new. This done, the candidates can be instructed to break the seals on the test booklet and begin.

There is a further important matter that needs consideration, and that is test security. Mention has been made several times of the need to keep the test secure. Security will affect the teachers in two ways: as teachers in the classroom, and in their capacity as supervisors of the test, for they will already (gloomily perhaps) have recognised themselves as the test supervisors. It needs emphasising, incidentally, that this book is not intended to be a supervisor's handbook; the duties of a supervisor are yet another aspect of the information that should accompany the objective test, particularly in the early stages of its use. Objective test security, then, has both administrative and educational implications, and of these the latter are the most important and are liable to arouse the greatest debate. To both candidate and teacher, objective test security will show itself most markedly in the fact that, after the test has been completed, the test booklet and the answer sheet (if they are not one and the same) will be collected and sent back immediately to the body responsible for constructing and scoring the test. This runs counter to existing practice by which question papers are available for discussion after the test has been taken, and can be purchased and used as the basis for practice tests and as one aspect of the teacher's preparation for future tests. Security also shows itself to both candidate and teacher in the arrival of the test as a sealed booklet and in the numbering of the booklet and the answer sheet. All this is done to ensure that the whereabouts of every copy of a test at a particular time is known, and that the chance of any preliminary leakage is kept to a minimum. It means, too, that the supervisor will have to check both answer sheets and booklets extremely carefully as soon as the test has been completed, and will need to comply with detailed instructions for their packing and despatch. Why is all this done; why are the teacher and candidate not allowed to see the test and discuss it afterwards? From an educational point of view, it is undesirable that a test which samples only a part of the total domain should be made generally available, as this might encourage practice on the questions that have actually been asked rather than encourage the teacher to teach the subject in order that the candidates can answer whatever questions may be asked. The fact that this kind of practice already happens in existing tests does not invalidate the principle. It is hoped also that this book and others like it, by describing the development and construction of objective tests, will reassure teachers that their purpils, if properly taught, will sit tests which sample adequately and measure systematically the content of the syllabus which is being covered and the skills and abilities which are considered appropriate to the subject concerned. It is, of course, only right that candidates and teachers should have the opportunity of seeing and trying out the various types of question that will be used in objective tests, and it is hoped that the necessity for this has been put sufficiently strongly in these chapters. Nevertheless, it is important to appreciate that these examples are intended to generate familiarity with the format and not to provide practice for the test itself. If this is realised, objective tests, particularly when used in combination with the more traditional approaches, will not have the harmful backwash effects that many fear. There are two further advantages that result from keeping the test secure: first, it does give the opportunity to repeat certain questions in successive years, and thus provides useful information on the performance of candidates over a period of time. This information can be of help in evaluating both curriculum development, as in the Nuffield schemes, and teaching techniques. The second advantage is rather more utilitarian. The development of 'good' objective items suitable for use in external tests, which measure worth-while abilities and which prove themselves in practice, is no easy matter, and if the test was not secure such items could not be used again for some time. Both practical and educational reasons would, therefore, seem to suggest that the maintenance of secure tests is both sound and realistic.

CHAPTER 6

Scoring the test

Objective tests can be scored either by hand or by means of a machine. While the future undoubtedly lies with machine scoring, particularly where widely taken tests are concerned, hand scoring will certainly continue to be used for smaller numbers; both methods of scoring will be discussed here.

When only one class is involved—in a classroom test, for example—scoring is likely to be carried out by the teacher by hand, and in this situation the test will probably have been answered by the candidates on the test booklet or paper itself. Even if a separate answer sheet has been used, it may well not be a specially designed sheet of the kind described in the last chapter. To score such a test all the teachers need to do is to provide themselves with a key and to mark the answers accordingly—though it is important, whenever possible, to have a sample check made on their marking. If the teachers wish to undertake any analysis of the results, this is a separate operation which should be carried out on the lines indicated in chapter 4.

Hand scoring for a widely taken test is, in essence, nothing more than a clerical operation, which requires to be properly organised under a supervisor who is in overall charge. The first step is to prepare a scoring key. For the tests supplied by their Cooperative Test Division, Educational Testing Service provide a special matrix stencil which is covered with perforated circles corresponding to the circles on the answer sheet. A sheet of carbon paper and a blank answer sheet are placed upon the matrix, and the three are clipped together, the order, from top to bottom, being answer sheet, carbon paper and matrix. The answer sheet is then marked up correctly and removed together with the carbon, all the marked perforated holes are punched out, and the key is complete. Anyone undertaking the clerical work of scoring objective tests can prepare a similar key very quickly and easily in this way, but all such keys should be carefully checked against each other and against the answers before being used. The method described is not, of course, the only one that can be used to prepare a key, but it is mentioned as an illustration. The following steps should then be carried out before the tests are actually scored:

1 Check each answer sheet to see that the candidates have filled in all the information that has been asked of them.
2 Check each answer sheet to see that no candidate has provided more than one answer to any question.
3 Clip the key to the answer sheet, both at the top and on one side.

If the checks in items 1 and 2 reveal any errors, the sheets should be put on one side and referred to the supervisor for a decision.

With regard to point 2, while a rule can be made that any question which receives more than one answer is automatically given no credit, there may well be occasions where a candidate has erased his original choice inadequately and has left two marks, one of which is darker than the other. In such a case the matter should not be left to the clerk's discretion, but should be referred to the supervisor.

After these steps have been completed the test should be scored and the total ringed in red on some convenient place on the answer sheet.

This procedure is then repeated. It is nothing more than a time-consuming clerical chore. A 10 per cent daily random check should be carried out on the work of each scorer, and if this reveals any errors, the complete day's work of that scorer should be re-checked.

Some hand scoring may be carried out on the answer booklet. Although the procedure is almost the same, it does present problems in the provision of a key. The Kenya Ministry of Education have devised an ingenious concertina mark key for scoring their primary tests. This fits inside the pages of the booklet and enables the scorer to check the candidate's answer against the key and record the total. There are endless possible designs for such scoring keys. It is worth mentioning, too, that the hand scoring of a booklet will almost certainly mean the transfer at some stage of marks from one sheet to another; this, of course, increases the possibility of human error and requires an additional check.

All that the procedures described have provided for those responsible for the test is the total raw score obtained by the candidate. No correction for guessing has been applied, no item analysis has been carried out, and no weighting of items has taken place. Separate operations will be needed for these. No attempt should be made to ask the scorers to do anything other than score, or the possibility of error will increase.

In discussing machine scoring one enters a different world, both in the speed and facility with which the scoring can be carried out and in the opportunities which are opened up by the possibility of linking the scoring process direct to a computer instead of transferring the information to the computer at a later stage. At the same time it is important, when talking to advocates of machine scoring, to disentangle what is at present being done from what it is intended to do in the future. With this word of warning, however, it is worth looking at the possibilities. In a lecture given in May 1967 in West Berlin, Professor E. F. Lindquist of the United States, whose Iowa Measurement Research Center is probably the most advanced in the world in this field, outlined what he considered to be the specification for the ideal scoring machine or optical scanner. This may be summarised as follows:

1   It should not restrict in any way the use of item types considered necessary by those constructing the test.
2   It should enable the candidates to concentrate as much of their time as possible upon the test itself and as little of their time as possible upon the instructions for and the methods of recording their answers.

3 It should provide an error-free, fast scoring service which can handle documents and cards of various sizes, while at the same time the machine would be simple to operate and easy to maintain.

4 It should be 'on line' to a computer; that is, the machine should feed the information obtained from the scoring process directly into a computer without any intermediate punching or recording stage.

After looking at this specification it is necessary to ask two important questions if such a machine is to become a practical proposition: first, what does the specification mean in practical terms and, secondly, to what extent is it being achieved in practice today? Both these questions can be answered by discussing in turn the four points summarised above.

1 The biggest single contribution to flexibility in the matter of the item types used would be the possibility of scoring the test booklet rather than a separate answer sheet, since the latter imposes considerable limitations upon item format. However, booklet scoring is not in itself enough. The ideal machine ought to be able to score:

a) items which permit the selection of more than one response
b) items in which certain of the responses are weighted or to which complicated scoring formulae are applied
c) items which permit a variety of free responses
d) inventories (for example, personality inventories) which require the respondent to underline sentences or phrases chosen from a list which might run into hundreds.

This illustrates a few of the item types that are already in use in tests, but which present difficulties as far as machine scoring is concerned. As far as the present position is concerned, machine scoreable booklets are in use in the United States, but they contain tests which make use of those item types, e.g. true/false, multiple-choice, matching, which can already be machine scored on an answer sheet; that is, the booklet is really a number of answer sheets. Further improvement can only result from improving the actual method of scoring, and this leads to the second point on the specification.

2   Here again, scoring the booklet itself is an immediate help, since it is easier for the candidates and will save their time. There is, however, more to the problem than this. The method of marking the correct answer is particularly important. At present, a square or circle or some other shape has to be filled in in pencil. How much simpler it would be if the candidate were able, by one single horizontal stroke of the pencil, either to underline or strike through the correct response. No special care would be needed. Allied with the question of marking is the question of erasure. At present it is necessary to rub out any incorrect mark very carefully and then fill in the alternative. If a single line was used, its erasure and replacement by another line would be both quick and simple. The marking of items is closely linked with the method of scoring actually adopted by the machine being used. The majority of machines at present in use adopt a density level of scoring; that is, a particular level of carbon density is selected by those operating the machine who take into account their experience of the darkness or lightness of the pencil marks normally made by candidates in tests. Any mark below this level of density is not accepted by the machine. If two or more marks of the permitted density or above are recorded, the item in question will not receive a mark. A far more reliable and fair method would be for the machine to scan all the marks made by candidates and to select the darkest mark for each item. In this way the candidate would not be penalised for failing to fully erase an incorrect answer; it would also mean that an ordinary pencil, and not a specially soft one, could be used. There are a number of possible methods of achieving this, and machines are already in use which carry out 'darkest mark' scanning, rather than using a density threshold. It should be noted that it would not be possible to machine score items in which more than one answer or response was correct if the scoring machine did not recognise a number of different levels of density.

3 Practically every word in the third part of the specification raises important questions and problems. 'Error free', 'fast', 'documents of various sizes', 'simple and easy to maintain' are all words and phrases which are a great deal easier to write down than they are to achieve in practice. The speed at which the machine has to work is bound up with the fourth point, the 'on line' connection with the computer, and also to a lesser extent with the actual number of candidates taking the tests to be scored. Bearing in mind the cost of computer time and the present capability of medium-range computers, one should be looking for a scoring capability of up to 60,000 sheets an hour. In achieving this, the greatest problem to be overcome is probably not that of scoring speed, but the provision of the necessary paper-handling machinery to cope with the demands made by the machine. It is also important to note that the realisation of error-free scoring will slow down the rate at which the machine works, since initially it will only be able to identify the errors and not to correct them.

Another aspect of fast scoring is the ability to scan or read both sides of an answer sheet or a booklet page at the same time. This obviously halves the time it takes to scan a given number of sheets. Scanning of both sides of a sheet is possible today but, since it is carried out by transmitted and not reflected light, it depends on the use of interlaced printing on the two sides of the paper. This has a number of disadvantages: first, it makes the printing of the sheet or booklet a very skilled and thus expensive operation; secondly, it requires the use of high priced optical quality paper; and thirdly, the candidates may be worried by the rather cramped design of the sheet, which results from the need to make the best possible use of the available space. One aspect of error-free scoring has already been mentioned—that concerning the identification of the marks made by the candidate. The simpler you can make the instructions and the marking procedures, the less likely is the candidate to make a mistake. The design of the machine can also help with the accurate scoring of sheets or booklets damaged by the candidate, or answers which the candidate has made rather carelessly, for example, underlining POITIERS instead of POITIERS, or marking (A) like this instead of like this (A). These tolerance limits can be built into scoring machines, although most of those in present-day use are not able to cope with such problems. Error-free scoring, moreover, means not only the identification of errors made by candidates in marking their answers but also errors made in the information which they have been asked to provide, such as their names and addresses. It is important to emphasise that if a wasteful punching process is not to be introduced, such information must also be written in a machine scoreable form, and this at present is both time consuming for the candidate and wasteful of space. For candidate JOHN B. SMITH (one of the shortest possible names) to write his name in this way, an absolute minimum of ten columns or rows is required. Each of these rows must contain every letter of the alphabet, and the candidate is required to black out the appropriate letter in each column. The whole edit programme which those operating the scoring machinery devise to deal with errors of all kinds is given the name of quality control. The edit programme of the Measurement Research Center in Iowa City includes the following: a check on the candidate's high school number, using the last number as a check digit; a check on all answer sheets or booklets which have scored very high or very low marks; a series of checks on the name and address of the candidate—for example, that the first blank in each column was filled in and that the words 'P.O. BOX' were automatically followed by a number and not a letter. If any of these or the other checks used reveal an apparent error, the form is 'checked out' for a visual inspection and the error corrected on a key punch device. Many more such checks could be carried out, and, indeed, need to be carried out if error-free scoring is to be achieved. One of the advantages of having the scoring machine 'on line' to a computer is that it permits computer editing of the data. Both the scoring machine and the computer together should be able to recognise clues to all errors that have been anticipated, and the computer can then print out a suspect error list which enables a visual check to be made of all 'suspect answer' sheets, which can then be altered.

The need for the scoring machine to be simple and easy to maintain may well not be attainable in so far as the first point 'simplicity' is concerned, but they are points which need bearing in mind because the requirement for qualified maintenance should be cut to the minimum if economy of operation is to be achieved.

4 The final point concerning the specification has been mentioned once or twice already. By making the machine 'on line' to a computer, one not only makes possible a quick and comprehensive edit programme, but also achieves economy, efficiency and speed in the scoring and in the subsequent provision of information to those who have taken the test. In particular, it avoids the use of intermediate card punching, which is time consuming and can easily lead to mistakes. Scoring machines are in operation which are 'on line' to computers, but they are rather the exception at present and a great deal of work is needed before the problems involved in achieving this part or indeed the rest of the specification for the ideal scoring machine can be solved.

The reader, particularly the teacher, may say with some justification that, while he can see the relevance of the previous chapters to his actual work, the problems of machine scoring will never affect him at all and that such matters are entirely the concern of large organisations concerned with test development and construction. The reasons for discussing this problem are two-fold: first, in any account of objective tests, the scoring of the tests as the final process needs consideration, and in this machine scoring plays a part today and will play an increasingly important part in the future. Secondly, we consider that machine scoring will in time make available to teachers information about their pupils which will be much more extensive and more quickly obtainable than the information they receive from existing tests. It will be for the teacher to see that this information is put to the best possible use both

inside and outside the classroom and for testing organisations
to tackle the problems of storing this information and making
it immediately available when it is required.

For the next few years in the United Kingdom the number
of tests that will necessitate machine scoring can be accom-
modated on a small number of machines, and if these are to be
used to the full there is a good case for the establishment of one
or two scoring centres to provide scoring and computer services
for testing organisations in return for a fee. The equipment
could also be used for scoring such things as market research
questionnaires and public opinion polls. There would thus be a
reasonable prospect of the cost of such equipment being re-
covered in a relatively short time.

CHAPTER 7

Educational objectives

We have been concerned in this book with a discussion of objective testing: what it is, how it can be developed and organised, and how it can be subjected to analysis so that it can be made into an effective and reliable measuring instrument for academic achievement. The objectivity arises from the objectivity of the scoring process, in contrast to the less objective marking of many other assessment procedures. It is important, however, to appreciate that objective testing is only one of a number of possible assessment procedures. We have discussed its strengths and weaknesses, and it would be a bold man who would advocate the replacement of all existing assessment techniques by this particular form of testing.

It is not possible to discuss objective testing, or any other form of assessment, without reference to the particular aims of a course, i.e. the curriculum objectives. The question 'What do we wish to test?' must precede the question 'What is the best type of test to use?' The first question can only be answered within the framework of the declared educational objectives of a course. What do we expect pupils who have been through the course to know and understand at the end of it? Do we expect them to have acquired certain skills, and if so what skills? Questions such as these help in the formulation of course objectives which are readily recognisable and clearly defined. Such a formulation goes beyond the traditional syllabus, which does no more than specify subject areas, in that it involves the specification of abilities and skills as well as knowledge of subject matter. Thus, in a school physics course we should expect the pupil to be cognisant of what one might call the 'vocabulary' of physics, i.e. concepts, definitions, laws, principles, etc. We should also expect an ability to apply this knowledge to certain physical situations and to explain certain physical phenomena. In addition, we should expect an understanding of experimental method and an ability to use this method in appropriate situations. Knowledge, comprehension, application and evaluation are all involved in the study of physics, although all are not necessarily involved at every level of this study. In this cognitive domain, we can see that many of the objectives outlined by Bloom in his (1956) *Taxonomy of Educational Objectives* have relevance to a course in physics. We should also expect the pupil to acquire certain practical or manipulative skills as distinct from appreciation of practical procedures; but this is outside the cognitive domain and beyond the scope of this book. A similar process of evaluation will enable the objectives of other courses to be defined in specific terms in much the same way.

It should not be thought that Bloom's taxonomy of educational objectives is the only taxonomy, or even the best that is available at present. R. L. Ebel (1965) gives a simpler taxonomy in his *Measuring Educational Achievement*, which many have found more relevant to their own course specification. The main thesis here is that a syllabus is not in itself a sufficient guide to the educational objectives of a course, and that a more comprehensive taxonomy is needed.

Now that we have defined the objectives of a course, the next stage is to determine how best these objectives may be assessed. We have seen that objective tests can be used with little difficulty to test factual recall or knowledge. Because objective questions do not require the candidate to write at length, they can be used to test knowledge over a wider range of the course than is possible in a predominantly narrative examination. This wider sampling of the course content means less temptation for candidates to try to 'forecast' questions, and less likelihood of the examiner putting a premium on the successful 'forecaster'. The chance element in assessment is thereby reduced and the approach to the examination by a candidate will thus be far less of a gamble. This must surely be educationally desirable. The obsession with past examination papers by pupils and teachers alike tends to focus attention on the wrong objectives. Instead of a course following previously defined educational objectives, it tends to be based on what experience has shown is likely to be examined. This is no reflection on teachers, but a criticism of deficiencies in current assessment practice.

Objective tests can be used to assess application and appreciation as well as knowledge, although such items are more difficult to construct and place heavy demands upon item writers. The ability to make an evaluation of a given situation may also be tested. The illustrative items in this book have shown how more than basic knowledge can be tested in this way, and Bloom and others provide further examples.

Objective testing cannot be used to test practical skills of the kind to be found in the sciences and technology, or oral skills in languages. In testing whether a candidate knows how to go about making a bookcase, for example, there is no guarantee that he can actually make one of reasonable quality. The practical sessions of many courses are designed to develop abilities and skills which cannot be adequately assessed in written form. If manual dexterity, care in making observations, the capacity to take pains in producing a first-class piece of work are considered to be relevant objectives in a course, then some kind of practical assessment becomes essential.

It would appear that many areas of assessment at the present time would improve in validity if a composite testing procedure were to be adopted. An objective test could be designed to test all the aspects which can be extracted from traditional narrative papers, such as factual recall, knowledge, comprehension and application. The narrative paper could then be confined to testing those objectives which require the candidate to write at greater length in order to marshal facts and to present arguments in a coherent manner. This is predominantly the area of value judgements. It is equally the area where the ability to analyse, synthesise and evaluate is at its highest level. Finally, some kind of practical or oral test is required to assess the practical or oral skills thought to be desirable.

An assessment procedure along these lines is likely to be of greater validity than many of the current procedures, in which the recall element is dominant and in which the testing of abilities when presented with an unfamiliar or new situation is virtually absent. Most candidates in physics can recall the traditional experiment to verify Boyle's law, and they can often make a tolerable showing in a practical test upon it. Many, however, may be quite unable to cope with an unfamiliar situation involving applications of the law in practice. If the ability to assess an unfamiliar situation is one of the declared objectives of the course, it should be tested; if it is not tested, then we can hardly complain if this omission has its effect on the course and the teaching methods employed. The Boyle's law experiment has been singled out for special mention because it is a particularly apposite illustration of the point.

What is true of the ability to apply experimental method in the sciences, as distinct from the ability to recall a familiar experimental situation, has its parallel in all courses of study. Can the history student think 'historically' at the end of the course, or can he only recall familiar dates, battles, etc.? Can the divinity student apply his knowledge and comprehension to contemporary situations, or can he only recall and recount what happened to St Paul on the road to Damascus? There is a real danger that if the recall element is dominant in examinations, the ability to memorise will become the *sine qua non* for success. This is not to argue that the ability to recall is not important, but rather that the other cognitive abilities are not being adequately tested. This again emphasises the need to define clearly those educational objectives which distinguish a particular course, and to ensure that they are satisfactorily tested. Curriculum content in practice, as distinct from theory, tends to follow the assessment pattern for the course. So, only too often, does educational methodology.

It is in this wider context of how best to assess the declared objectives of a course that objective testing should be regarded. It is an additional form of assessment to consider along with existing forms, to be chosen only when considered most appropriate for assessing the particular objectives one has in mind. For other objectives, alternative forms of assessment may be more suitable. That one form of assessment should prove to be satisfactory for all types of objectives is most unlikely.

The adoption of objective testing in those areas where it is considered that it will be appropriate requires very careful thought. Enough has been said in this book to show that item construction is not something which can be dashed off in an odd moment, put on paper, scored and forgotten. The scoring of objective tests is certainly easy and straightforward; the construction of worth-while items is not. This raises the question of how best to provide training for teachers and others concerned with test construction; how to give them, in effect, the practice and expert criticism which they will need to become proficient. Not everyone will eventually write good items, but there is no doubt that a large number can become moderately proficient if they receive help. This problem is at its most acute at the present time, since there are few professionally constructed objective tests in existence.

For the large organisation with professional staff the best method of training is probably by means of a residential item-writing workshop. This is, in essence, four or five days' item writing under expert supervision in which items are constantly being criticised and revised. In this way, the basic techniques of item writing can be quickly acquired if an individual has a particular talent in this direction. Such workshops are, however, expensive and require trained staff. Moreover, since the organising body hopes to make use of item writers identified as being 'good', it is likely that those attending will be as far as possible pre-selected from among those who have some experience of item writing already or who seem likely to prove successful at it. It is not, therefore, a solution which is likely to benefit in any substantial way the teacher who would like to acquire an additional testing technique for use in the classroom. It also runs the risk of making the whole process appear too much of a mystique in which only the specially selected and trained can participate.

Even for examining boards, while an occasional workshop is invaluable, there is a lot to be said for a rather less formal approach in which groups of the board's examiners and committee members, after drawing up the specification for the test, also write items and provide the criticism themselves. The editorial experience at least should come from the board, and the measurement and statistical expertise either from an outside consultant or from the board's own research unit, where such exists. Once again, however, this approach will probably not reach the teachers in the schools. What can be done for them? There appears to be little or nothing, at least to start with, while they remain on their own. It is essential that there should be more opportunities for meeting with others so that ideas can be pooled and criticisms exchanged. The universities, colleges of education and local authorities might provide such opportunities by holding discussion groups or even workshops, and by encouraging teachers in this way to meet and work in groups. This approach is already being tried out with success in curriculum development. One of the best ways of evaluating curriculum development is by means of periodic classroom tests, and proficiency in objective testing could be a valuable complement in this respect. The possibility of providing two or three regional consultancy units which can provide expert advice to the teachers within the regions is well worth considering if wasteful duplication of effort and the loss of valuable time is to be avoided—a point which existing examining boards might also consider with advantage.

Whatever the difficulties, there is no doubt that the experienced teacher has the greatest potential for successful item construction. It has already been stated, in discussing the construction of multiple-choice items, that the distracting options need to be plausible, not simply wrong. The teacher is far more familiar with the kind of misunderstandings and misconceptions pupils have in any given subject area than the subject specialist who has never taught. It is in this region of common 'howlers' that the best distractors may be found. The following item is based on the experience of the author (RBM) in teaching and examining the practical appreciation of the potentiometer in physics.

A physicist wished to compare the e.m.f.s of two cells and set up the potentiometer circuit shown below. The cell of e.m.f. E_1 was connected to the potentiometer wire AB of length 50 cm. The cell of e.m.f. E_2 was connected in series

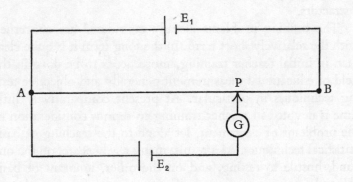

with a galvanometer to an adjustable contact point at P. Initially no balance point was found and this was traced to the fact that:

A   the potentiometer wire AB was too short

B   the cell of e.m.f. E_2 was connected the wrong way round

C   the e.m.f. of E_2 was greater than the e.m.f. of E_1

D   the galvanometer was incorrectly connected in the circuit

E   the internal resistance of cell of e.m.f. E_2 was too high.

On one occasion a candidate at a practical examination set up this circuit and failed to get a balance point. He asked for another potentiometer with a wire of length 100 cm. When asked why he wanted a longer wire, he replied that he had almost got a balance at the end of the 50 cm. wire and the additional length would make all the difference! He also stated that he never had this trouble at school because all the potentiometers had 100 cm. wires! This experience, which was by no means uncommon, provided the distractor A. All the other distractors have their origin in experiences of this kind. They form the best source of plausible distractors in that, at some time, somewhere, a pupil actually thought in this kind of way. There are parts of a course where pupils voice the same misconceptions year after year, and these provide even better distractors.

The training problems already considered are concerned with the relatively short term. In the long term it is quite clear that, in initial teacher training, more needs to be done in the field of educational measurement generally and objective testing techniques in particular. At present comparatively little time is devoted in teacher training to serious consideration of the problems of assessment, let alone to the teaching of basic statistical techniques. As a result, many teachers are, on the one hand, hostile to testing, and on the other, ignorant of basic principles concerning the use of test scores, as, for example, the need to reduce marks or scores to a common scale if one wishes to compare and add marks or scores in any meaningful way. The aim of courses in education is to help the teacher or future teacher to be a more effective teacher. This lack of any appreciation of educational measurement, however, means that the majority of teachers cannot realistically assess their own effectiveness and are handicapped when they become interested in research. The revision of courses on education in this respect seems long overdue, although there are now signs of a greater awareness of this need.

The reader who has a knowledge of programmed learning and who has studied the structure of various programmes will have noticed a similarity between such programmes and objective test questions. In both cases the student is invited to make a response and to choose from a number of options. In the learning situation the choice of the wrong option leads to an explanation of why it is wrong and the student is returned to the original question to try again. In this way the student progresses through the programme. If the programme is to be effective, the alternative choices need to be as plausible as the distractors in objective testing, and based on actual misconceptions that students have had frequently in the past. This similarity means that objective questions may be used in a teaching or learning situation and not confined simply to testing. Where the distractors are well founded upon the teacher's awareness of pupils' difficulties they serve to highlight those difficulties, and the teacher can help the pupil to appreciate why they are wrong.

It is as important a part of education to know why things are wrong or limited as to know why they are right or comprehensive. The idea that distractors or false options in objective testing or programmed learning are giving pupils false notions which would otherwise not have occurred to them does not appear to be particularly realistic. We have long since abandoned the view that the teaching of morals involves keeping the pupil in ignorance of wickedness: indeed, the appreciation of the good would be meaningless without an equal appreciation of the bad. We must not push this analogy too far, but to advocate maintaining a discreet silence to protect pupils from making mistakes or acquiring false notions would seem to defeat the intended purpose.

The scientist T. H. Huxley once remarked of the undergraduates of his day that they came to the university to pass examinations rather than to increase their knowledge and understanding. He said of them, 'They work to pass and not to know. But science has its revenge. They do pass, and they don't know.' In fairness to the undergraduates one might question what exactly their examinations were testing. If the examinations were such that students could pass without possessing the understanding and abilities Huxley thought desirable, it would seem that those examinations were not matched to the educational objectives of the undergraduate course; and in such a case one cannot help feeling that the fault lay with the examiners rather than with the students.

This need to be quite clear about the objectives of a course cannot be overstressed, and the test constructor must be familiar with these objectives before beginning his work. If it is decided that a course is concerned with application, analysis, synthesis and evaluation as well as knowledge and comprehension, then a test which is made up of items in the proportion of 70 per cent knowledge and 30 per cent comprehension is clearly not matched to the course. If candidates know this, it will not be surprising if the other objectives are neglected and they pass the test without necessarily having any ability at application, analysis, synthesis or evaluation. Thus it is that the form and content of the final test can strengthen or distort the declared objectives of a course, making curriculum development a living reality or simply an academic exercise. It is in the hope that objective testing may assist in the increased realisation of educational objectives that this book has come to be written.

References and suggested further reading and study

ANASTASI, A. (ed.) (1966) *Testing Problems in Perspective*. Washington D.C.: American Council on Education.

BLOOM, B. S. (ed.) (1956) *Taxonomy of Educational Objectives: Handbook 1, Cognitive Domain*. London and New York: Longmans.

EBEL, R. L. (1965) *Measuring Educational Achievement*. Englewood Cliffs, N.J.: Prentice Hall.

Educational Testing Service *et al.* (1963) *Multiple-Choice Questions: A Close Look*. Princeton, N.J.: Educational Testing Service.

GARRETT, H. E. (1958) *Statistics in Psychology and Education*. London: Longmans.

GERBERICH, J. R. (1956) *Specimen Objective Test Items*. London: Longmans.

HAWES, G. R. (1964) *Educational Testing for the Millions*. New York: McGraw-Hill.

HOFFMAN, B. (1962) *The Tyranny of Testing*. New York: Crowell Collier Press.

LINDQUIST, E. F. (1951) *Educational Measurement*. Washington D.C.: American Council on Education.

Secondary School Examinations Council (1964) *The Certificate of Secondary Education: An Introduction to Some Techniques of Examining*. Examinations Bulletin No. 3. London: H.M. Stationery Office.

STANLEY, J. C. (1964) *Measurement in Today's Schools*. Englewood Cliffs, N.J.: Prentice Hall.

THORNDIKE, R. L. and HAGEN, E. (1961) *Measurement and Evaluation in Psychology and Education*. New York: John Wiley.

VERNON, P. E. (1956) *The Measurement of Abilities.* 2nd edition. London: University of London Press Ltd.

VERNON, P. E. (1960) *Intelligence and Attainment Tests*. London: University of London Press Ltd.

VERNON, P. E. (1964) *The Certificate of Secondary Education: An Introduction to Objective-type Examinations*. Schools Council Examinations Bulletin No. 4. London: H.M. Stationery Office.

WOOD, D. ADKINS (1961) *Test Construction.* Columbia, Ohio: Charles E. Merrill.

Tests and Measurement Kit (1963) Prepared by Evaluation and Advisory Service, Educational Testing Service, Princeton, N.J.

Most of these books are concerned with discussion of the problems of educational measurement and objectives. The book by B. Hoffman is probably the best known critical attack on objective testing.

Index

Acknowledgments

The authors and publishers would like to thank *Punch* for permission
to reprint the cartoon on p. 29, and the Oxford and Cambridge
Schools Examination Board for permission to reprint the item on
pp. 20 and 21 from the O level Nuffield Physics Paper I of June 1967.